The Homemade Wedding Cake

The Homemade Wedding Cake

NATASHA COLLINS

MURDOCH BOOKS
SYDNEY · LONDON

Contents

PART TWO: THE PROJECTS 62

For Mum and Dad

WELCOME TO
The Homemade Wedding Cake

*An unspecified number of years ago (insert the relevant figure,
depending on how old you think I am...) I married a lovely man.
I can honestly say that it was one of the best days of my life,
and a day that I remember with huge affection,
albeit a little hazily now through the mists of time.*

Back then, things were very different: when I got married the internet hadn't been invented.... Well, it existed, but it wasn't as commonplace and easily accessible as it is now; people really only used the web for work, rather than leisure (nobody could afford the dial-up costs to spend time looking at kittens, babies laughing or people falling over). That meant that there were no wedding bloggers, no crafting sites and definitely no Pinterest; nothing that the brides of today take for granted as sources of inspiration...

At the time I was working as a textile designer in a London studio, and I was the owner of a (head)strong aesthetic, so I felt that I needed to be heavily involved with creating projects for my big day. I decided that, where possible, I would not be sourcing readymade products for the event; this was most definitely going to be a DIY wedding, with my own stamp on things. So I designed and made the invitations, the order of service and the wedding favours; I created banners to decorate the church and marquee; I roped in friends and family to help with the flower arrangements and to prepare the food for the reception, and that included the cake. Not for me a traditional wedding cake with intricate piping, overloaded with swags of sugar-paste flowers or, heaven forbid, plastic columns! Instead I persuaded my mum to help, and she baked three delicious fruit cakes, which we covered with fondant and then decorated by sprinkling real petals over the top and sides. Fortunately one of my aunts is brilliant at making sugar-paste flowers, so she made a little posy for the top of the cake that tied in with my spring flower theme. It felt perfect, it fitted in well with the feel of the day, it helped us to keep under budget and, most importantly, it tasted great.

My husband was less involved in the planning, it has to be said. He had just one job, which was to pick the music for us leaving the church. He picked a song that had been on the radio a lot when we first met—without realising that it had since been used as the title track for the film *So I Married an Axe Murderer*—and he couldn't understand why everyone was sniggering as we walked back up the aisle. Despite this (in case you were wondering) we are still happily married and I still consider him to be a lovely man!

Let's fast-forward to the present day, where I am in the full flush of a new career, working as a professional cake artist. One part of my job is teaching classes on how to paint on cakes, and frequently in these classes there are students who are there because they are making their own wedding cakes (or have volunteered to make one for a friend or family member). I am always slightly in awe of their bravery. Even though I did make my own wedding cake, (and when I say 'I' there, I obviously mean my mum) with the benefit of hindsight I realise that I really didn't have a clue about the many potential issues that could have spelled disaster for my cake. When I look back now, after many years' experience working in the cake-decorating profession, I pale at the thought of my lack of knowledge: I can't remember if we doweled the cake, and I do wonder about the flowers we used as decoration... were they poisonous? (If you were at my wedding and ate some cake I can only apologise for this oversight. I hope you are still in rude health, and I'm pretty certain they were fine to eat!)

It was while I was trying to imagine the stress that my students were feeling about creating a cake for someone's special day that the idea for this book popped into my head. I began to mull over the thought of a guide for those plucky souls who have decided to make a homemade wedding cake.

This musing intensified when watching a televised baking competition. As the finale, the competitors had to make a showstopping wedding cake in just six hours. Six hours! Now, I have to say even as a professional I would find it very hard (if not impossible) to make something amazing in this time – my cakes take me three days to make at least. A couple of the contestants were overambitious with their designs and decoration, which caused them problems, and I thought: if these experienced bakers can fall at this hurdle, how would everybody else cope? A bride (or indeed groom; let me note here that I'm not assuming that my own husband's lack of involvement in wedding matters is representative of all men...) could be spending hours diligently collating a mood board of their ideas, maybe looking at images of what they imagine to be a handmade wedding cake, and believing that they could achieve something similar. However, as a professional cake maker I recognise that most of these cakes are skillfully made, but designed to have a deliberately rustic appearance.

My specialty (as a professional cake maker) is painting onto fondant, and one of the reasons I had for pursuing this particular niche was that it best suited my skills: I was a qualified illustrator but I had no formal sugarcraft training. This meant I couldn't pipe or make sugar-paste flowers, so out of necessity I had to find ways to cheat and make cakes look great without expensive equipment or training: tips that can help someone with a wedding cake to make who is big on ideas and inspiration, but is also perhaps a little short on experience. I also know firsthand that many brides, grooms, maids of honour or close family members have much more to worry about in the run up to a wedding than to spend three days baking, covering and decorating a cake. So I have written this book to show you how to create a fabulous looking cake while keeping your sanity (and that of the people around you)!

BEFORE YOU DON AN APRON

Congratulations! Woohoo! Cue the confetti and the popping of Champagne corks. You are getting married! This is one of the most exciting times of your life, and there is so much to look forward to; not only one very special day, but a future with the exceptional person that you love. It's a time to gather your friends and family around you, as you celebrate this special commitment to your sweetheart.

But first comes a great deal of organisation. You will have a thousand and one different decisions to make about your wedding day, but—as you are holding this book in your hands—I'm guessing that you have already made the decision to bake and decorate your own wedding cake, even if you may be wondering how to go about that. I'm here to help...

There are many considerations to take into account and I'll talk you through them all. But first you need to put yourself into the right frame of mind. If you had decided to pay a professional to make your cake, you would meet them for a consultation, where you would spend some time talking about yourself and your wedding day, discussing your cake requirements and trying out samples. As a cake maker myself I love this part of the job; I get to meet people at one of the happiest times of their lives, and my clients always really enjoy the time too. So, before you start reading, treat yourself to your own private consultation. Make a cup of tea (or even better, pour yourself some champagne), sit down for a quiet few hours, relax, pamper yourself and have a good read.

THINGS FOR YOU TO CONSIDER

MOTIVE
While it may be just conjecture on my part, I am going to assume that there are many different reasons why someone might want to make their own wedding cake, and all of these motives will have implications on the final design of the cake. Perhaps you really love baking, have lot of experience and want to make one special item yourself for the big day. Maybe you are on a limited budget for the wedding (I know I was) and making your own cake will help keep things under budget. Possibly you have a strong artistic side or are a crafter, and you want to create something really personal. Let's consider these scenarios in turn.

THE BAKING EXPERT
Baking a wedding cake is obviously a more complicated process than if you are making a cake for Sunday tea, and usually they are much larger than an everyday cake

(unless you are secretly eloping and therefore only need a cake for two).

You really don't want to be up at dawn on the morning of your wedding, with your apron on and hair full of flour, baking up a storm. So I have created all of the recipes in this book to be perfect even when made in advance, allowing you to enjoy the big day. Many of them can be made five or six days in advance, or alternatively can be frozen: I'll outline at the beginning of each project how suitable they are for the freezer.

Being a fabulous baker doesn't necessarily equate to being a good decorator, and a wedding cake is more complicated than just producing a good bake: careful decorations can transform a relatively simple cake into a stunning centrepiece. Bear in mind that a tiered cake needs to be correctly stacked to prevent toppling and cracking, but this is a fairly simple process, so don't feel anxious. Even if you are already a baking wiz, this book will teach you the skills that will help you to create a confection that will delight your guests.

THE BUDGET-CONSCIOUS BRIDE
The first thing to say is to be prepared for a wedding cake to cost, gram for gram, a little more than a normal cake would, depending on the type of cake you choose to make. For example, a rich chocolate cake (which is basically pure chocolate, with just a hint of flour and butter waved over it) will typically cost you twice as much as a more basic vanilla sponge cake, though you will find recipes for both in this book. A homemade cake doesn't necessarily mean a cheap cake, although obviously it will still be significantly cheaper than a professional cake, but you will need to consider your budget before you decide on which recipe you want to make. I can't give you specific costs for each cake, as ingredient costs fluctuate and their prices will vary from region to region, but I have given you an idea of where the price of the cake would fall on a scale that runs from low-cost to expensive.

THE ARTY CRAFTER

If you have a passion for crafting then you should already have lots of expertise that will help when it comes to decorating the cake, but you may be a little lost with the baking side of the project. You will find that each project is rated for baking and decorating difficulty separately, so that you can choose something suitable for your skill set.

Use this book as the touch paper to ignite your own vision and create a really individual cake. You will find it easy to mix and match aspects of projects. You are creative, so make it personal by mixing things up your own way! If you are too nervous to bake your own cake, or are an artist with a paintbrush but a disaster with oven gloves, then why not charm a friend or family member to do this part for you, leaving you with the happy task of decoration?

BRIDEZILLA... OR BRIDECHILLA?

Another important consideration is your personality: are you a totally laid-back type who can happily cope with last minute problems? Or perhaps you are organised and efficient, already three steps ahead and armed with a colour-coded wedding folder? Perhaps one of the 'right up to the last minute' projects is for you.

Or do you get stressed and flustered very easily? Maybe you have a million other projects you have committed yourself to on the week of your wedding? If you are the easily stressed type then please don't choose a project that can only be completed on the actual day.

Every project in this book includes a timetable so that you can see how much time each part of the process will take, and will give a timetable for when the cake should best be decorated and set up in relation to when it is going to be eaten.

Confession time: I can now admit that I was probably something of a bridezilla before I got married. I knew exactly what I wanted, I knew how I expected everything to look, and I was determined to make it all happen perfectly. With the benefit of hindsight, I probably could have been

a bit more laid-back and relaxed, but it's not easy to realise that at the time. If you are aware that you may fall into this particular trap, then do consider carefully the type of cake you should make. You are probably better off making one that you can bake and decorate in advance, so that you are not faced with any last-minute disasters, leaving you the peace of mind to spend the day without any unnecessary worry about icing, decoration or sugarcraft.

By contrast, if you are very easygoing and happy-go-lucky, then do consider a cake that may need a bit more in the way of last-minute baking or finishing. But please take into consideration everything else you are committed to in the run up to your wedding: it doesn't matter how easygoing you are, if you don't leave yourself enough time to actually make the cake, it isn't going to happen. Bear in mind the people who are supporting you through this exciting time: are they up to some last-minute mucking in? Never be afraid to ask for help: I'm sure that you can find a host of helpers willing to whisk and craft for you. Perhaps buy the ladies on your hens' night an apron as a gift, so that they get the message in advance...

Finally, think about your plans for the day itself. Are you scheduling a morning of head-to-toe beauty treatments, making sure that you literally glow? If so, do you have plenty of friends or family who could set up the cake while you are being pampered? Are you getting married at home, or at a venue where you can set the cake up the night before? And what type of environment is the cake going to be sitting in: is it totally tropical, icy cold, or in between? You will find advice on storing and displaying the cakes with each project, so that you can choose the best one for you.

Some cakes can be made well in advance, and then on the day you can just place them on a cake stand and they're ready to go. Others that use fresh flowers or fruit may need to be set up no more than four hours in advance. That might mean that you need to call on the help of a good friend who can set your cake up for you while you are having photos taken, or if you have planned a very casual day then you may be happy to do it yourself.

THE CAKES

part one

CHAPTER ONE

Baking a wedding cake

*Before you decide on a cake to bake you need to think about the day itself.
There are many considerations you will want to take into account: such as, do you
want to be baking the day before the wedding; will you have time to set up the cake
on the actual day; what will the temperature of the room be? This chapter will explain
the issues you should think about and how to resolve any potential problems.*

FOR THE BRIDE OR GROOM WHO LIKES TO BE PREPARED

I know that I would definitely come under this heading. I am the type of person who handed in their school and university projects a week before the deadline. I like to have everything sorted and ready long before it is needed. I don't pull all-nighters! If I was getting married now I would want to bake a cake that I could make and decorate in advance, so that if there was a disaster (and these things do happen) I would be able to quickly make or find a replacement.

If you can recognise yourself in this description then you need to consider which cake to make. Obviously the best type of cake, in this instance, is a fruit cake. They are traditionally made three months in advance, then fed with brandy or another liquor each week. They can be covered a few weeks in advance and decorated then too. This is the perfect recipe for an organised bride; however, there is very little demand for a wedding cake based on fruit cake. Most of my clients opt for a less-traditional sponge cake, or a rich chocolate cake. If they do want fruit cake they just have one tier. The issue with fruit cake is that because it is quite a heavy cake you need to use it as the bottom tier and so the majority of your served portions of cake will be fruit.

Traditionally the top tier of a wedding cake would be saved for the first baby's christening. If you attempt to put a top tier of fruit cake onto tiers of a lighter cake you really risk the bottom tiers cracking.

If you do want to serve a little bit of fruit cake, then considering making an extra cutting cake. This is a cake that is kept separately from the main cake (normally out of sight, in the kitchen) that can be cut up and served with the rest of the cake.

A sponge cake that is covered with fondant will also keep slightly longer. I have made a cake like this two weeks in advance and it was still fresh at the wedding; however, there are other pitfalls to consider and my advice would be to stick to a fruit cake if you want to bake well ahead.

FOR THE EASYGOING COUPLE

Some cakes need to be made at the last minute. Normally I would make sponge cupcakes either the evening before an event or on the day. For this reason I haven't included a recipe for sponge cupcakes in this book, but if you really did want to make these you can always bake them in advance and freeze them (more of this later). I have

included a recipe for chocolate cupcakes. These cakes are actually best made a day or two in advance as time will improve their flavour.

There is a real trend for naked cakes at the moment, and they do look beautiful and rustic. While they can be made a few days in advance and filled, once they are displayed they really only should be standing for a maximum of four hours. If you are laid back about the organisation details, and not likely to be bothered by last-minute preparation, this type of cake may suit you. The recipe I have included in the book for a naked carrot cake has been specially formulated to have a longer shelf-life.

INGREDIENTS

The joy of a homemade wedding cake is that you know it has been made from scratch, not from a packet, and you have been able to carefully source the ingredients yourself. Where possible, opt for more expensive brands as they will create a more flavoursome cake. If finances are not a pressing issue, always opt for the best.

However, if you are making your own cake as a means to save money don't worry if you have to buy inexpensive ingredients: even using lesser-quality products your cake will taste absolutely delicious.

BUTTER

All of my recipes use unsalted butter. It is better to add the salt separately if needed, as you are in control of the exact amount in the cake. Cheaper butter has a higher water content, which can make the flavour more insipid. Top bakers prefer to use a good French butter as this can really make a difference to the cake flavour. The more expensive brands will include less water and are also whiter in colour, which helps to produce a whiter buttercream.

SUGAR

Icing sugar (confectioners' or powdered sugar): unrefined (or raw) icing sugar will produce frosting with a richer, rounder flavour; however, the colour will not be as white as that produced by using refined icing sugar. So if the project calls for a white icing then stick with the refined type. I find that icing sugar tends to clump a little in its package, so I would recommend that you sift it before you use it.

Caster sugar (superfine, ultrafine, bar or baking sugar): a finely ground sugar well suited for baking cakes. I usually prefer to use an unrefined (raw) sugar as this will impart a richer flavour, especially if you are creating caramel; however, if I am making something such as a lemon cake, I prefer a refined sugar as the caramel flavour of the unrefined sugar can overpower the tartness of the citrus, although this is purely a personal viewpoint. If you cannot source caster sugar then substitute granulated sugar (see below), which you can whizz up in a food processor for a few seconds to achieve the fine grains.

Granulated sugar (regular or white sugar): this is a coarser grain of sugar than caster sugar. It's used to add a crunch to biscuits, and can be used in baking as a substitute for caster sugar.

Brown sugar (light or dark, muscovado or molasses sugar): all brown sugars retain a certain amount of molasses after refining; the darker the sugar, the higher the molasses content. Brown sugars are great for adding to gingerbread cakes or biscuits and cakes with a stronger caramel flavour; however, don't be tempted to substitute them for caster sugar in other recipes without some testing and experimenting first, because using these sugars can affect flavour and baking time and the cake can burn more easily.

Golden syrup (light treacle): if you cannot source golden syrup then you can use corn syrup or glucose syrup.

EGGS

All of the recipes in this book use large eggs, and where possible try to use organic eggs. For meringues, Swiss meringue buttercream and crystallising flowers, use pasteurised egg whites to prevent the risk of salmonella and also save the waste of all the egg yolks. Pasteurised egg whites are usually found in the chiller cabinet with ready-made pastry; they may be in a container (usually

like a milk carton) with a conversion chart on the side
to show how many tablespoons of the mixture you will
need to make up the equivalent in egg whites.

FLOUR

You will find many different brands available in your
local supermarket. If your budget allows, go for a more
expensive brand as this will be finer and will make lighter
cakes. I tend to use self-raising flour rather than making
up my own with plain (all-purpose) flour and a rising
agent, mainly because it's quicker, easier and I have never
had any problems with my cakes rising. If you do prefer
to make your own then add 2 teaspoons of baking
powder for every 150 g (5½ oz) of flour used. Self-raising
flour can lose its rising properties as it ages, so make sure
that you use flour that is well within its use-by date (the
same goes for baking powder). When baking biscuits, use
plain (all-purpose) flour; if you can, use one of the more
expensive brands. Traditionally, the flour is sifted over
the cake mixture; however, I find that whisking the flour
in a bowl with a whisk or a fork before adding it to the
rest of the mix results in exactly the same outcome.

RICE FLOUR

This is a flour made from milled rice that is used
to add crunch to biscuits. You can substitute finely
ground polenta.

COCOA POWDER

Use unsweetened cocoa powder rather than drinking
chocolate mixture and make sure that you don't use
a fat-reduced version. You need all that fatty goodness
to create a beautiful flavour.

CHOCOLATE

Use a good-quality dark chocolate rather than 'cooking'
chocolate. Steer clear of anything that is described as
'chocolate flavoured'. Couverture is the best type of
chocolate to use when baking, although you may have
to get this from a specialist online supplier. Couverture
chocolate is often sold as drops or chips, which enable
the melting process to work more quickly and evenly.
If you are using a solid chocolate bar then chop it up
with a knife into much smaller pieces.

Most supermarkets stock good-quality dark
chocolate, which you should find either in the baking or
confectionery aisle. The percentage of cocoa solids in the
bar is really a matter of personal taste. A chocolate bar
with a high percentage of cocoa solids—say 75–90%—
will give you a stronger, richer taste. A high cocoa solids
content doesn't necessarily equate to a bitter taste (this
is more to do with the roasting of the cocoa beans) but
do try a little of the chocolate before you use it in the
cake, to make sure it is to your taste. If you prefer a
sweeter flavour then go for chocolate with a lower cocoa
content, although it should be at least 54% for the cake
to remain chocolatey; however, if you are making
ganache, do not use chocolate with more than 54% cocoa
solids, as the ganache will split more easily (don't worry
if this does happen as it will still taste great, it just won't
look so good).

For recipes using white chocolate, go for a really good
high-quality product that actually tastes of chocolate
rather than just added fat.

I usually melt chocolate in a microwave, on a very
low setting, initially for a minute and then for bursts
of 30 seconds, stirring frequently. Alternatively, you can
melt the chocolate in a bain marie; this is a heatproof
bowl that fits in the top of a saucepan, which is filled
with gently simmering water (but not enough so that
it touches the bowl).

FRUIT

For flavourings choose fruit that is at the peak of its
ripeness. Under-ripe fruit will be hard and sour, but
over-ripe fruit can go off very quickly.

Dried fruit: you can use any type of dried fruit in a fruit
cake recipe. The conventional varieties used are sultanas,
currants, raisins, cherries and dried peel (orange and
lemon). I would always recommend the more expensive
products as the fruit will be plumper, juicier and contain

fewer pips; however, most supermarkets sell bags of generic mixed fruit that are normally very cheap and, for those working on a small budget, they are your best option.

When baking with cherries I prefer to use natural ones rather than the brightly dyed version, as they have a rounder fuller flavour; however, if the cherry is being used for decoration then the bright red glacé style has a more pleasing aesthetic.

You can easily source tubs of ready-cut peel: the peel tends to be quite small and hard, but perfectly adequate. You can also buy a version of whole peel that is not precut; you chop it up into the required size. This product tends to be less pithy and tastes fresher than the ready-cut variety.

You can use any selection of dried fruit, such as apricots or figs, but do remember that the higher-quality fruit has less chemicals used to dry them or preserve their colour, so they (and therefore your cake) will taste better.

Citrus fruit: All of the recipes in this book that contain citrus utilise the zest of the particular fruit as well as the juice. Because chemicals are sprayed onto the fruit, do buy organic fruit if you can afford to; if you can't, make sure you wash the fruit well before you use it. In addition, choose wax-free fruit: companies add a layer of wax onto the surface of citrus fruits to preserve them longer during shipping, so obviously if you are grating the skin to use the zest you are also adding a sprinkling of wax to your cake. To release the maximum amount of juice from a citrus fruit, roll the fruit on the work surface, applying firm pressure with the palm of your hand. This crushes the fruit inside and releases more juice when you squeeze it. Zest the fruit with a fine grater and add this to the butter and sugar before you start beating them. This pummels the zest and releases even more of the fruity oil.

Apples: to create an apple purée you will need to use baking or cooking apples rather than an eating variety. When cooked these apples reduce down into a purée adding flavour and moisture rather than a crunchy texture.

Bananas: use very, very ripe bananas to bake with. The peel should be practically black. If a banana is under-ripe, heat it gently in the microwave then make sure it has cooled

before you add it to the mixture. On the other hand, if a banana ripens too quickly, freeze it (with the skin on) until you need it.

NUTS

Any nuts that you use in a cake or for decoration must be well inside their use-by date as they can go rancid and taste bad. I would also recommend that you don't use any nuts if the packets have been open for a long period of time, even if they are within the use-by date.

SPICES

Old spices can lose their flavour, so make sure all spices are within their use-by date and that they still smell pungent.

SALT

Some recipes will require normal table salt (fine salt). For others you will need a flaky salt: there are many different varieties available, and it can also be known as kosher salt.

CONSERVES

I never put fresh berries into a cake as a filling; it is fine if you are serving a cake immediately but after a few hours the juices in the fruit seep into the cake and make it soggy. So to add fruit fillings I use conserve (a jam or jelly). If you wish you can make your own conserves, but if you are not confident in your jam-making skills or you are subject to time constraints then by all means buy a ready-made conserve (I do). If your budget will allow, choose a better brand as these will have more fruit and less sugar; alternatively, hunt down unusual and tasty flavours at farmers' markets or from local producers.

FLAVOURINGS

Always use natural flavouring where possible, as the cake will taste much better. Natural vanilla extract used rather than synthetic essence will impart a richer, fuller flavour to the cake. I particularly like to use vanilla bean paste as it adds the little black flecks of vanilla into the mix as well as a delicious flavour. There is something about the visual stimulation that makes the cake taste even vanilla-ier (don't mock me: my spell check suggested 'vanillaier', which makes it a real word and one I now intend to use in everyday conversations)! Vanilla extract usually includes alcohol as one of its ingredients, so if you don't want to use this then substitute the seeds of one vanilla pod for each teaspoon of the flavouring. Use a sharp knife to split the pod lengthways, then open it up and scrape out the seeds into the mixing bowl. Don't discard the pod, as you can add this to a jar of sugar to make vanilla sugar, or drop it in a pan of hot milk while you bring it to the boil, take it out and then use the vanilla-flavoured milk for a truly scrumptious hot chocolate.

When buying any flavouring always choose a bottle that states 'extract' rather than essence. Essence is often a chemical product whereas extract comes straight from the source.

LIQUOR

There was once a time when some wines were deemed good enough only for cooking with, but thinking on this particular subject has definitely changed. If you are using an alcoholic liquid in your baking, do make sure that it is a good brand and good enough to drink.

In all the recipes you can change the type of liquor to suit your taste, for example if you are making a fruit cake you don't have to stick with the traditional brandy. Whisky or even Cointreau (orange-flavoured liqueur) will produce an equally delicious cake, as long as you choose a product that is flavoursome. A liquor such as vodka or gin will not add anything to your baking.

MILK

You can use full-fat, semi-skimmed or fat-free milk in any of these recipes.

CREAM

The recipes will specify which type of cream to use. Thin (pouring) cream has a fat content of about 35%, while thick (double) cream has a fat content of about 45%.

BUTTERMILK

This is usually found in the dairy aisle of the supermarket alongside the cream. If you can't source buttermilk you can make your own by mixing one part milk with three parts yoghurt.

MARZIPAN

While you can make your own marzipan, a ready-made version will taste just as good and be much easier to use. I prefer to use the natural-coloured version rather than the yellow, but either is good.

FONDANT (SUGAR PASTE)

When I refer to fondant I mean sugar-paste icing that you roll out and use to cover a cake. I always use commercial, ready-made, ready-to-roll fondant, which most supermarkets now stock, or you can buy larger quantities from specialist cake-decorating suppliers; however, the supermarket packets should be sufficient for the projects in this book. You can make your own fondant, but unless you are very experienced I would advise that you make it easy for yourself and buy ready-made fondant.

BAKING EQUIPMENT

Unless you have plans to kickstart a new career in cake decorating after making your wedding cake, you really don't need to go and buy a cupboardful of specialist equipment. If you are fortunate enough to have a friend or family member who dabbles in cake decorating, play the wedding card in the hope that they will be kind enough to lend you some of their equipment. Do not worry if you don't have a baker friend, you should be able to make most of the projects in this book with the tools you already have in your kitchen.

OVEN

Each oven will vary in its temperature scale, so most professionals will use an oven thermometer to check that it is reaching the correct temperature; however, you do not need to go out and buy one. It's to be hoped that you will have a fair idea about your own oven, and if it cooks hotter or cooler you can adjust the scale accordingly.

I would suggest that you practise—do a dummy run—of the cake in advance, even if it is just one layer: make notes about cooking times for when you cook the actual cake. When you are baking the cake do keep a close eye on it as it nears the end of the cooking time to make sure it doesn't overcook. Most ovens have a hot spot in one area, so if you are baking multiple cakes keep an eye out for one cooking quicker than the others. You can turn cakes or move them around to ensure even cooking, but don't do this until you are at least three-quarters of the way through the cooking time.

If cakes are disturbed early on in the cooking process they can sink in the middle and take on a dense texture. This is why you don't test whether a cake is ready until near the end of the cooking time. I recommend using a fan-forced oven when baking cakes, to produce a more even temperature throughout the oven. If you are using a fan-forced oven, remember to set the oven temperature 20°C (35°F) lower than the temperature that is recommended in the recipes.

SCALES

It really is better to use electronic scales, which are much more accurate than the traditional type: accuracy is key when baking. You can find fairly inexpensive electronic scales in most supermarkets.

BOWLS

It may seem obvious, but for a larger cake in particular you will need a really big mixing bowl; at least 4–6 litres (140–210 fl oz/16–24 cups) if you are mixing more than one layer at a time.

WHISKS

If you already own a standing electric mixer that you use when baking, do use it in your normal fashion for the projects; the same goes for a food processor. I suspect that many readers will only have a handheld electric whisk, so I have created these recipes with this in mind, which is why most of the cakes are baked one layer at a time. If you don't own an electric whisk, you can still make these recipes with just a wooden spoon or a hand whisk, and on the plus side it will firm up your arms ready for the big day!

MICROPLANE GRATER

This is a very fine grater that will grate the zest from a citrus fruit without tearing into the pith. It is fab for grating nutmeg and ginger too; however, you can use a normal grater.

ZESTER

This tool creates strips of zest from a citrus fruit. If you do not have one then pare the peel from the fruit with a knife and finely slice the peel into strips.

SAUCEPANS

An everyday saucepan will be suitable for most of these projects; however, if you are making caramel you will really need to use a heavy-based pan to prevent burning. Alternatively you can use a heavy-based frying pan or even a heavy wok. If you don't have a heavy-based saucepan then use a normal one and, if it does burn on the bottom of the pan, pour out the caramel without scraping the bottom of the pan and it should still taste delicious.

CAKE TINS

As a professional baker I usually bake each tier of a cake in one tin, then trim the top and cut the tier into three layers for filling and icing. Partly this is to ensure uniform cake layers but mostly because I can then get on with other jobs while the cake is in the oven. A large cake baked this way can take up to four hours to cook through and it is a riskier way to bake as the top and sides of the cake can burn while the inside can be undercooked. So for most of these recipes you will find the ingredient quantities are for just one layer of a cake tier. You will have to bake at least two and usually three layers to create one tier.

You can choose to bake three layers at once if you have three tins of the same size: I realise that it is probably only professional cake decorators who would own a whole set, but you can beg, steal and borrow from friends and family, or find a cake-decorating supply shop that will hire out tins. If you only have one tin of each particular size then you will have to bake one layer at a time. If you are making a project where all three tiers of the cake are the same flavour then you can mix and bake one layer of each size tier at the same time, and this will save you a lot of time.

BAKING STRIPS

These are insulating strips that go around the cake tin, to prevent the edges of the cake from burning and help the cake to bake evenly. You can buy them from specialist baking suppliers, or you can use a strip of newspaper or an old tea towel (dish towel): these strips need to be soaked in water before you put them in the oven to prevent any fires.

BAKING PAPER (BAKING PARCHMENT)

Line tins and baking trays with this to make it easy to release the cakes or biscuits after baking. Do not use greaseproof paper, as this will stick to the cake.

CAKE TESTER

This is a long, thin metal rod that you insert into the centre of the cake to check that it is cooked. If it comes out clean, the cake is ready. You could also use a skewer or even a cocktail stick in the same way.

CAKE RACK (COOLING RACK)

This is a wire mesh platform raised on short legs that you rest the cake on when you turn it out from the tin. It will allow the cake to cool quickly, preventing it from continuing to cook in the tin. The open structure of the rack also prevents the bottom of the cake from becoming soggy. If you don't have a cooling rack then use a clean oven shelf (removed from the oven) as they usually have the same structure.

CUTTING CAKES

PORTION SIZES

Before you decide on the cake you wish to make you need to think about the portion numbers you will require. It is said that 20 per cent of wedding guests do not eat any cake; personally, I cannot conceive of an opportunity where I would pass up free cake, but everyone is different (if a little strange). If I were making a cake for my own wedding I would cater for every guest, as there will always be a few who go back for seconds (and, if I were at the wedding, possibly even thirds or fourths.)

THERE ARE TWO DIFFERENT WAYS OF CALCULATING PORTION SIZES:

* Traditionally a party portion size is a 2.5 cm (1 inch) square finger. These are served as small taster pieces, usually at a wedding where dessert has already been served. This may seem very small, but remember these cakes are quite tall, so each person will still receive an acceptable amount.
* Dessert portions are usually 2.5 x 5 cm (1 x 2 inches) and are often served with berries and cream.

Note   *The number of portions given for the cakes in this book are all party portions.*

Of course, you don't need to adhere to these portion sizes: if you think that your guests would prefer larger slices of cake then you can make your own calculations. The easiest way to do this is make a paper template the diameter of your cake and then divide it into the portion size you require to show you the number of people it will serve.

It's often difficult to create a wedding cake that serves the exact number of portions needed, so you will have to decide on a size that roughly suits your numbers. You may end up with a slightly bigger or smaller cake than you need (personally I always go for a bigger cake, as having some extra cake left is not a major disaster but more of a total win) and you will find plenty of people hanging around for a few days after the big event who will happily dispose of it for you. Most cake can also be frozen if you want to save the extra for after the honeymoon, as long as it has not previously been frozen. If you are freezing a fondant-covered cake, take off the fondant first.

CUTTING CAKES

Sometimes couples do not want an extravagantly large cake; they would rather have a more modest two- or three-tier cake, but that may not feed all their guests. So I create a 'cutting cake' for them. This is a cake that may be the same flavour as the main cake but is undecorated. It sits out of view, usually in the kitchen, and is cut up and served with the main cake to produce the number of portions required. For the purposes of the projects in this book I am assuming that you are not a professional baker and are not used to stacking (tiering or merging) a cake, so I have not included any instructions for cakes larger than three tiers; therefore, if you need extra portions to serve all your guests, I would suggest making a cutting cake to add to the numbers.

HOW TO BAKE YOUR WEDDING CAKE

PREPARATION

Preparation is the key to remaining stress-free when you are baking your wedding cake. You don't want to be whirling around the kitchen like a dervish only to find that you have forgotten to buy a vital ingredient. So make yourself a checklist of everything that you will need, both ingredients and equipment, and check it all off before you start baking.

Before you start baking you also need to prepare the cake tins. Each tin will need to be greased and lined with baking paper, to make sure that the cake will come out cleanly.

GREASE AND LINE THE CAKE TIN

1. Use a very small amount of butter to grease the base and sides of the tin (if you add too thick a layer it will cook into the cake and create a greasy film on the outside).
2. Place the cake tin on top of a piece of baking paper and draw around the circumference (or sides, if it's a square tin). Cut out this shape.
3. The width of the strip of baking paper that you need will depend on the cake you are baking. If you are baking one layer of the cake at a time the strip will need to be 6 cm (2½ inches) wide; however, if you are baking each tier as one large cake then the strip should be 9 cm (3½ inches) wide. The length of the strip should be the circumference of the cake tin plus a 2 cm (¾ inch) overlap. Make a fold along the length of the strip 2 cm (¾ inch) up from the bottom of the strip.
4. Make a series of cuts from the bottom edge of the strip up to the fold approximately 1 cm (⅜ inch) apart.
5. Place the strip in the cake tin with the fold running around the edge of the tin and the fringing on the cake base. The butter should make it stick: if you find that the overlapping pieces aren't sticking, smear a little butter on the back of the overlap so that it sits flush to the tin.
6. Then place the baking paper circle (or square) into the base of the tin.

PREPARE THE INGREDIENTS

Before I start to bake I weigh out all my ingredients into smaller bowls, to save time and mess (just the ingredients for the actual cake, as you will make the icing or frosting at a later time).

Dried fruit: to make the most delicious fruit cake possible you should prepare dried fruits the day before you bake. Mix all the fruits required in a heatproof bowl and pour boiling water over them. Leave to soak for 10–15 minutes: this allows the fruit to really plump up so that it will absorb any added flavouring more easily. After the allotted time, pour the contents of the bowl into a large sieve or colander to drain as much water as possible. If you don't have a suitable piece of equipment for doing this you can use a clean chopping board held flush to the top of the bowl and then move it slightly to make a small gap to allow the water to exit but none of the fruit. Put the fruit back into the bowl and add the alcohol (or fruit juice if you prefer). If you've forgotten to do this step the day before, don't panic: just soak the fruit in boiling water as described above and drain thoroughly. You need to cool the fruit down or it will melt the batter. If you are cooking a large fruit cake (or three cakes) then this may take some time. You can speed up the process by spreading the fruit onto large baking trays and drizzle the alcohol or juice over it all. Add the fruit to the mixture when it is thoroughly cooled.

Butter: needs to be at room temperature. This is the conventional way to describe it, although obviously if you live in the tropics with no air conditioning then your room temperature is going to be very different to somebody baking in wintery Europe. What this well-worn phrase means is that the butter should be soft enough to beat easily. If you put the butter in a bowl and find that you are having to stab at it to break it into small pieces, it is too cold. Imagine a packet of cream cheese straight from the fridge: that is the consistency you want. If you have forgotten to take the butter out of the refrigerator then you can warm it through slightly in the microwave, but keep a beady eye on it and be very careful that it doesn't melt. If the butter is melted instead of at room temperature it will affect the texture of the cake, which can become dense and doughy.

GREASE AND LINE THE CAKE TIN

1

2

3

4

5

6

MIX THE BATTER

Flour: weigh the flour into a bowl, one that leaves enough space to give it a good whisk. Add any spices, salt or raising agents and then whisk it with a fork or a hand whisk to incorporate air and break up any lumps. If you have really lumpy flour then you may need to sift it (picture 1).

Cocoa: in my experience most cocoa powders can contain hard lumps, so sift it first.

Eggs: should also be at room temperature. If you keep your eggs in the refrigerator then take them out at least an hour before you need them. If you forget to do this, fill a bowl with warm water (not hot, as you don't want boiled eggs) and leave the eggs in the water for about 5 minutes. I break all my eggs into a separate bowl first and whisk them together: this makes it easier to incorporate them into the cake mixture in a controlled manner (picture 2).

Every time you handle eggs you should wash your hands (think about where they came from) so by cracking them all at once you are saved from making multiple bathroom trips!

To separate eggs, I crack the egg in two then hold the egg yolk in one shell while the egg white pours out into the bowl; you may have to swap the yolk into the other side of the shell to separate all of the white. Some people pour the egg into the palm of their hand and let the white trickle through their fingers while they keep hold of the yolk. If you have a technique that works for you, stick with it.

Flavouring: if the cake mixture includes flavourings such as apple purée or caramel, make these in advance to give them time to cool down. If you add something warm to a batter it will melt the mixture and create a disappointing texture. The same principle applies to melted chocolate, although you will need to use this before it starts to set. If you are making your own flavourings such as elderflower syrup or lavender sugar then make them a month or so in advance to give time to allow the flavours to develop.

LET'S GET BAKING

It's time to bake. You may be baking together as a couple; perhaps one of you has taken on the mantle of 'baker'; or maybe you are hosting a 'bake my wedding cake' party,

in which case don't drink too much champagne before it goes in the oven. Your mood can really affect your baking, so I always play lively music while I'm baking and switch to a more chilled style when I'm decorating and need to concentrate. A happy heart makes a happy cake.

Each recipe in this book includes a method, but do spend some time reading through these more general tips before you begin. As I mentioned previously, I married some time ago, and my fabulous husband Paul is something of a genius at writing. I frequently ask him to edit my recipes, blog posts, press releases—in fact, anything that the public will see—to make sure I haven't embarrassed myself with poor choice of words. One of the first recipes he edited for me used the term 'cream together the butter and sugar'. He is not a baker and was very puzzled as to what this actually meant. 'It just means beat them until they look creamy, everybody knows that!' I expounded. He patiently explained to me that as a complete novice baker he absolutely couldn't make sense of it, and so I started to consider the baking terms that I unthinkingly throw around, that are not actually very explanatory. So I will attempt to make these terms more understandable.

Preheat the oven: this is pretty much self-explanatory. Before you start mixing the batter, set the oven to the correct temperature to ensure that by the time you put the cake in, it will have reached the precise temperature required. If you put a cake in a cold oven, it will not bake evenly all the way through and may sink in the middle.

Cream together the butter and sugar: weigh out the butter and sugar and put them in a bowl that is large enough to let you beat them properly (if using citrus fruit, add the zest at this stage as well). Then use an electric whisk to start beating them together. You need to move the whisk around the bowl, making sure that it reaches the bottom and the side of the bowl, so that every little bit is incorporated into the mixture. If you are using a hand whisk you will probably need to beat the mixture for about 10 minutes to ensure it reaches the desired consistency. If you are going old school and using a wooden spoon it may take even longer (picture 3). When you start beating, the mixture will be quite firm and—depending on the type of butter you use—

probably tinged yellow. As you beat the mixture, it will become fluffier and paler until it is practically white (picture 4, previous page), then it has been creamed!

If you find that your bowl is slip-sliding away, get more purchase by putting a tablecloth underneath while you beat.

Add the eggs: as mentioned previously, you should crack all the eggs into a bowl and beat them together (a fork is sufficient for this). While you are still beating the creamed butter and sugar with one hand, use the other to gradually pour in the eggs in a steady (but fine) trickle. Of course it is much easier if you have a pal to pour while you beat and hold the bowl still (picture 5, previous page).

If the mixture separates or curdles: sometimes when you add the eggs into a cake mixture the different elements don't come together quite in the manner you intend, and they can curdle. You will see the butter forming tiny clumps with the egg as a barrier around them. Don't panic! It really isn't the end of the world: your cake will still cook and be delicious. The best tip I can give you if this happens is to add a small amount of the flour (another reason why it's good to have it already weighed out) as this will encourage all the ingredients to blend together.

Fold in the flour: when you get to this stage lay aside the whisk or wooden spoon and take up a large metal spoon (at least tablespoon size) or a plastic spatula. Add a small amount of the flour and slide the implement of choice about a third of the way down between the side of the bowl and the mixture then bring the spoon up and over, folding the mixture into itself; repeat this process until all the flour has been incorporated (picture 6, previous page). This helps retain the air incorporated into the flour when whisking it and creates a lighter cake. This technique can be used for anything that is folded in, such as dried fruit purée, caramel or egg whites. You can also use a figure-of-eight movement.

Ribbon stage: this is a term used usually when whisking egg yolks (or whole eggs) together with sugar. The mixture should triple in size and become very pale and fluffy. After 10 minutes it should have reached the 'ribbon stage': if you lift the beaters out of the bowl, a thick ribbon of the mixture should form which should take 3–4 seconds to disappear back into the batter (picture 7).

Stiff peaks: this a term used when beating egg whites and meringue. After greatly increasing in volume, the egg whites pass through the soft peak stage, where the peak flops over when you lift the beater, to stiff peaks (picture 8): the mixture should be glossy and white, and when you lift the beaters out of the bowl a peak should form that does not flop over. The traditional way to test if you have reached the correct stage is to hold the bowl of meringue upside-down over your head: if your head remains egg-free then it's ready!

Caramelise the sugar: it is really important when you are making caramel, or any sugar syrup, not to stir the mixture in the pan. You can give it one or two stirs at the most, but I prefer to swirl the pan a little. Stirring creates sugar crystals and if you find that instead of a beautiful rich, luscious caramel you have a pan of white powder this is what has happened. There is no coming back from this, you just have to throw it away, wash the pan and start again.

Put the cake batter into the tins: if you are mixing three layers of a cake at the same time then you need to ensure the batter is evenly distributed among the tins. If one tin is fuller than another it will take longer to cook and the thinner cake may burn. If you are very precise, weigh the tins to make sure exactly the same amount goes into each. I am not a very precise person, so I tend to count out spoonfuls (picture 9). You will be trimming each layer before you stack them, so a little discrepancy isn't a problem.

As soon as the tins are filled put the cakes into the oven. The raising agents start to work immediately after mixing: if you leave an uncooked cake sitting out for too long it will not rise when baked. This is why you preheat the oven.

Test to see if the cake is ready with a cake tester: a cake tester (or skewer) should be inserted into the very middle of the cake because this is the part of the cake which cooks last. When you pull it out, it should be totally clean (picture 10). Sometimes you may find small particles that will look like cake crumbs, because they are cake crumbs! This is okay and also means that the cake is baked. If the tester is covered in cake batter, quickly close the oven door and wait for another 5–10 minutes before trying again. When a cake is ready the top should be a lovely golden-brown colour, although with chocolate or ginger cakes, for example, it is hard to tell by colour if the cake is cooked. If you lightly press a couple of fingers on to the top of the cake it should feel firm but springy, if you feel any wobble the cake isn't ready yet.

Leave the cake in the tin for 10 minutes: once the cake is cooked and out of the oven, leave it in the baking tin for 10 minutes. This gives the cake a little bit of time to settle so it won't crumble when you turn it out.

Turn the cake out: the best way to do this is to put a wire cooling rack upside down on top of the tin and then, with the tin and rack held firmly together in both hands, flip it upside down. Wear oven gloves while you do this. If you find that the strip of baking paper is deeper than the cake you may have to quickly whip it off at this point, to prevent the cake breaking into pieces. Now carefully turn the cake over so that it cools the right way up. You can place a second wire rack (if you have one) on the bottom of the cake and flip the cake over: this will prevent it cracking as it cools. When completely cooled, remove any baking paper, wrap in plastic wrap and store in an airtight container.

RIBBON STAGE   7

STIFF PEAKS   8

BAKING THE LAYERS   9

TESTING THE CAKE   10

GENERAL METHODS

MAKING MODELLING PASTE

Sprinkle gum tragacanth (CMC or Tylose) onto the work surface and knead it into ready-to-roll fondant. Knead well for 10 minutes, form the fondant into a ball, then cover it with a couple of layers of plastic wrap and set it aside overnight. (If using CMC or Tylose the paste will be ready to use immediately.) You can make the modelling paste in advance and keep it in a freezer until needed: just take it out a few hours before you need it to let it thaw.

MAKING ROYAL ICING

Mix the icing sugar and meri-white powder together, then slowly add the water and whisk vigorously. When the icing has become a thick paste, stop adding any more water. If you feel the icing is too thin you can add some more icing sugar.

CARAMELISING SUGAR

Put the sugar into a saucepan that has high sides and a thick base. Put the saucepan over low to medium heat until the sugar has dissolved. DO NOT STIR! If you stir it the syrup will crystallise and you'll have to throw it away. The sugar will start to caramelise around the edge of the pan first. You can very gently pull the caramelised sugar into the centre of the pan or swirl the pan to make sure the sugar doesn't burn. The sugar will turn a rich red–brown colour.

MAKING CARAMEL

1. Caramelise the sugar using the method above.
2. When all the sugar has dissolved, take the pan off the heat and add the butter (if using it). You may find it bubbles up a bit so be careful. Then carefully add the cream.
3. Stir the cream into the caramelised sugar. You may find that the caramel contains big lumps of toffee: if so, simply return the pan to the heat and stir until smooth.
4. Add the salt (if using) and stir well, leaving the caramel to cool in a heatproof bowl. The caramel can be made up to two weeks in advance and kept in the refrigerator.

MAKING SWISS MERINGUE BUTTERCREAM

1. Fill a saucepan one-third full of water and bring it to the boil, then turn the heat down so that the water is gently simmering. Place a heatproof bowl onto the saucepan so that it catches on the sides—it should be just bigger than the pan so that it sits snugly on top—and anything you add to it will be heated by the steam below. Make sure that the bottom of the bowl doesn't touch the water.
2. Put the egg whites and the sugar into the bowl. Stir the mix until all the sugar has dissolved: when this has occurred you should be able to rub a little of the egg white in between your thumb and fingers and not feel any grittiness from the sugar. Take the bowl off the saucepan and transfer the mixture to the bowl of a standing electric mixer (if using one). Using the fastest setting, beat the mixture for around 10 minutes, until it has reached the stiff peak stage (see page 33).
3. Add the butter one piece at a time and beat it in well. Don't worry if at some stage the mixture starts to look curdled; keep beating and the butter will incorporate into the meringue. Once all the butter has been added, beat for another few minutes.

MAKING GANACHE

1. Put the chocolate in a large heatproof bowl. If you are not using buttons or drops then make sure to chop the chocolate into very, very small pieces.
2. Put the cream into a saucepan and bring it to the boil. Pour it over the chocolate.
3. Use a wooden spoon to beat the mixture together until the chocolate has melted and the two ingredients have combined together to create a beautiful glossy ganache.

MAKING SUGAR SYRUP

1. Put the sugar and water in a saucepan over medium heat. Don't stir, just give the pan a swirl.
2. When all the sugar has dissolved, turn up the heat and bring the syrup to the boil.
3. Once the syrup is boiling, take the saucepan off the heat and add any citrus zest (if using). You will need to use the syrup while it is still warm, but you can make it in advance and gently reheat it when layering the cakes.

1

3

2

4

2

3

CHAPTER TWO

Trimming, filling and covering the cake

After baking the cake, leave it overnight to allow the crumb to firm up.
Then you can start the first process in decorating.

EQUIPMENT

CAKE LEVELLER

This is a piece of equipment that will make each layer of the cake totally flat and level. It looks a bit like a cheese cutter (picture 1, overleaf). The simplest version of this particular piece of equipment is actually fairly cheap; however, I totally understand that you may never use it again, and there is a 'make do' way to achieve the same effect. You will need cocktail sticks (toothpicks), a tape measure (or ruler) and a large knife, preferably a serrated one. Take a layer of the cake and measure 2 cm (¾ inch) up from the base: insert a cocktail stick into the cake at this point, Repeat at intervals of around 5 cm (2 inches) all around the cake. Then, using the cocktail sticks as a guide, use a serrated knife to trim away the top of the cake (pictures 2 & 3, overleaf).

PASTRY BRUSH

Each layer of cake should be brushed with sugar syrup to help it stay moist. The easiest way to do this is with a pastry brush: if you don't have one, carefully drizzle the syrup onto the surface with a spoon, then use your fingers to spread it over the cake. If you are using a pastry brush with bristles, rather than a silicone version, do check for loose bristles left on the cake.

PALETTE KNIFE

Also known as a spatula. Most people will own a large one for turning pancakes or for spreading and lifting. Cake decorators use smaller palette knives, usually 10–12.5 cm (4–5 inches). These are great for adding filling between layers and spreading it around the edge. You can also substitute a larger palette knife or a butter knife but use the flat side rather than the serrated edge.

TURNTABLE

This could be a tilted or untilted turntable. It's a flat, round surface that rotates in both directions on a stable base. Using one makes it easier to fill and decorate a cake, but you can create a wedding cake without a turntable, or you can create a makeshift turntable by placing a cake board on top of a cake tin; however, you will need to be extra-vigilant to make sure that the cake doesn't fall off.

CAKE SCRAPER

This is a flat rectangle of thin plastic or metal that is used to create perfectly straight sides when covering the cake with buttercream. You can use anything that is long and flat as a substitute: I have found that one of the best alternatives is a child's 15 cm (6 inch) clear plastic ruler.

CAKE DRUMS

These are cardboard cake boards thick enough to carry the weight of a cake, even a tiered cake. They are usually 12 mm (½ inch) thick. The cardboard is covered with a foil coating, normally silver or gold, although I've also seen metallic pink or blue. I always cover these boards with fondant icing and hide the edge with ribbon: my pet hate is an uncovered board under a beautiful cake.

CAKE BOARDS

These are similar to cake drums, in that they are also made out of cardboard and covered with foil; however, they are much thinner than drums. You can buy single thickness boards 2 mm (1/16 inch) thick, double thickness boards 3 mm (1/8 inch) thick or 4 mm (3/16 inch) thick boards. None of these boards would be suitable for use as the baseboard, as they are not thick enough to hold the weight of a cake. They are used to create internal support for tiered cakes.

SMOOTHERS

These are flat paddles with handles that you use to create a beautiful smooth surface on fondant icing. Place the flat surface of the smoother onto the surface of the fondant and, with even pressure, move around the surface of the cake until it is perfectly smooth (or as near as you can get). You can, however, achieve an acceptable finish by simply using the palms of your hands.

ROLLING PINS

To roll out fondant icing and cookie dough you will need a rolling pin about 46 cm (18 inches) long, preferably a plastic version. Wooden rolling pins can leave marks and indentation on the surface of the fondant; however, for the projects in this book a few marks will not be an issue. You will find it useful to use a small 15 cm (6 inch) long rolling pin when rolling out modelling paste; again, you will be able to make do with a larger wooden rolling pin, if that is all you own.

SPACERS

These are long thin plastic strips that you use when rolling out fondant icing, marzipan or cookie dough to get an even thickness. I use 5 mm (¼ inch) spacers. You can make your own spacers from strips of wood or plastic. You can also roll out fondant icing without using spacers: after you have rolled it out run the palm of your hand over the surface to find any bumps and dips. Smooth these out with your palm or a smoother.

COCKTAIL STICKS (TOOTHPICKS)

Any type is suitable, wooden or plastic.

DOWELS

To support the tiers of a cake you will need to use dowels. These are available from cake-decorating suppliers, and can be plastic or wooden; either type will be suitable for these projects. Plastic dowels may be solid or hollow (like thick straws) and can be cut easily with a serrated knife, or even with scissors (if you have the hollow type). Wooden dowels can be cut with wire cutters or a small hacksaw, so if you only have a knife or scissors to hand, go for one of the plastic types. You can also use drinking straws but make sure you are not using the bendy parts.

SPIRIT LEVEL

A small spirit level is a handy tool to test whether a surface is completely horizontal. You may be able to find some cake-decorating suppliers that sell spirit levels, but your local DIY store will definitely stock them (just make sure it is a small one, rather than a metre-long tool)! Keep this purely for cake decorating purposes. You can do without one and just use your eye to see if the cake is level. Sometimes I compare the top of my cake to lines on my kitchen tiles to see if it is level (but this is assuming the tiles are level in the first place).

EDIBLE INK PEN

Find these in specialist sugarcraft shops, online or in some craft shops. Use them to mark the dowels when cutting them. You can substitute an ordinary felt-tip pen but make sure you don't get any ink on the cake and that you wipe it off the dowels before inserting them.

LEVELLING A CAKE

ICING A DRUM

You do not have to use a cake drum underneath the cake. The cake can be set straight onto a stand or plate; however, using a drum will make it infinitely easier to work on the cake, to transport it and to set it up and possibly prevent a last minute disaster.

You can place the cake on a board for transportation then remove the board and transfer the cake to a stand, but it's tricky. To make it easier, you can place a board the same size as the cake underneath before covering the cake (as you would for one of the higher tiers) and then cover it when you add the fondant or buttercream. If you were to do this I would recommend another smaller board under the main one, to make it easier to pick up and put down. For example if the bottom tier is a 25 cm (10 inch) cake, glue a 20 cm (8 inch) cake board in the centre under a 25 cm board. Stand the cake on the 25 cm board and cover as normal.

If you use a drum that is larger than the cake, it will protect any decoration on the side of the cake while you are transporting it. I usually use a drum that is 5 cm (2 inches) larger than the diameter of the cake (this ratio seems visually appealing), so a 20 cm (8 inch) cake would be presented on a 25 cm (10 inch) cake drum. For a tiered cake, use the size of the bottom tier to calculate the drum size.

Glue a cake board that is 5 cm (2 inches) smaller underneath the larger drum to make it easier to pick up and set down the cake. Then, at least one day before you cover

the cake, prepare the cake drum. This is to give the fondant icing on it sufficient time to firm up, making it less likely to mark or dent when you put the cake on top.

METHOD

1. Sprinkle the work surface with cornflour (cornstarch) or icing (confectioners') sugar. Knead the fondant icing for a few minutes until it is pliable and smooth. Don't overwork it or it may crack when you roll it out.
2. Roll out the fondant using spacers (or alternative: see page 38), so that it is slightly larger in diameter than the drum you want to use. If there are any air bubbles on the surface of the fondant, prick them with a pin and smooth out with your palm.
3. Lightly moisten the cake drum with water.
4. Lay the fondant on top of the drum and smooth it over with smoothers or the palm of your hand. Trim the edge of the fondant to the size of the drum using a sharp knife.
5. Smooth out the fondant again. Then trim the edge very carefully, keeping the blade of the knife flush to the board. Run your finger around the edge of the fondant to smooth it down.
6. Cover the edge of the drum with a ribbon. (It's best to do this after the cake has been placed on it and all the decorations are done, to prevent any staining.) I find that 17 mm (⅝ inch) wide ribbon is a good size for covering both the drum and fondant edges. »

Quantity of fondant required for cake drums (you'll find that this leaves you with excess fondant to trim off).

15 cm (6 inch)	180 g (6¼ oz)
18 cm (7 inch)	250 g (9 oz)
20 cm (8 inch)	300 g (10½ oz)
23 cm (9 inch)	400 g (14 oz)
25 cm (10 inch)	550 g (1 lb 4 oz)
28 cm (11 inch)	660 g (1 lb 7½ oz)
30 cm (12 inch)	780 g (1 lb 11½ oz)

Amount of ribbon required to cover the edge of cake drums

15 cm (6 inch)	50 cm (20 inches)
18 cm (7 inch)	57 cm (23 inches)
20 cm (8 inch)	66 cm (26 inches)
23 cm (9 inch)	73 cm (28¾ inches)
25 cm (10 inch)	81 cm (32 inches)
28 cm (11 inch)	89 cm (35 inches)
30 cm (12 inch)	99 cm (39 inches)

Place a strip of double-sided adhesive tape around the edge of the drum and adhere the ribbon to the tape. If you are using a particularly thick ribbon or one made from natural or rougher fibres, you may need to use a hot-glue gun to attach it. Alternatively, you could cut a strip of patterned paper or fabric to cover the edge. I have been using washi tape more and more as it comes in such fabulous patterns and is really easy to use.

LAYERING A CAKE

After baking, store the cake overnight before you layer and fill it, as it needs this time to settle. If you try to fill it before this time has elapsed then you may find it too crumbly to work with.

Each layer of the cake should be the same depth, as this creates a great-looking cake, especially after it has been cut for serving. Measure the depth of the thinnest layer (if you are making a three-tiered cake you may have up to nine layers). This will be the size to which you will need to level all the layers. Either use a cake leveller or cocktail sticks and a serrated knife (see the equipment list, page 37).

Each cake in the project section will be filled with different ingredients: some with buttercream, some with ganache and others with preserves. The specific quantity for filling each cake is included in the recipes, but the general principle will be the same.

To create strong support, each tier of the cake will need to be placed on a cake board at this point. The bottom tier can be placed on an uncovered cake board and then transferred to the iced drum once the covering has been applied; however, middle tiers and top tiers need to be placed on thin cake boards before filling and crumb coating. This will give the cake support when it is dowelled. The board needs to be the same diameter as the cake, so 20 cm (8 inch) cake should be placed on a 20 cm board. These should not be the thick cake drums: the thinner boards will not add too much height to the cake.

Place the cake on the board at the filling stage, so that it becomes incorporated into the cake; the covering you then apply will completely cover the board as well. This means that when all the tiers are merged, you should not be able to see any of these boards at all.

Check at every stage (both when filling and covering the tiers with buttercream) that each cake is level. If the cake isn't level at any point, add some more buttercream to the lowest area to build it up.

FILLING A CAKE

1. Before you fill the cake, brush off any loose crumbs and then brush sugar syrup (or an alternative) on to the cut sides of each layer. This will help to keep the cake moist for longer. Take the layer that was the top of the cake, turn it over and place it on a cake board that is at least 5 cm (2 inches) larger than the cake so that the part of the cake that was at the top will be the base of the finished cake (this means that the roughest surface—the one that you have cut—will be hidden at the base of the cake). Stand the cake and board on a turntable if you are using one.

2. To add a layer of preserves, use a palette knife (or alternative) to create a ledge of buttercream around the edge of this first layer. This will hold the preserves in place and stop them from mixing with the frosting on the outside.

3. Then spread the preserves over the cake up to the buttercream ledge. If a cake recipe calls for two layers of buttercream, then add a dollop of buttercream instead of the preserves at this point.

4. Take the middle cake layer and place it carefully on top of the filling on the bottom layer.

5. Add a good dollop of buttercream in the middle and spread it to the edge.

6. Next take the remaining layer, turn it upside down and place it on top of the cake (this gives you a good flat top and a nice sharp edge to work with).

Use this technique if the cake is being filled with preserves, ganache, buttercream or Swiss meringue buttercream. The steps are the same for two- or four-layered tiers.

BUTTERCREAM

COVERING A CAKE

CRUMB-COAT

This is a thin layer of frosting spread over the sides and top of a cake to seal in any crumbs on the surface: it is the base on which you add fondant or a thicker layer of frosting. The method is the same for buttercream, Swiss buttercream or ganache.

1. Spread a layer of buttercream over the top and side of the cake using a palette knife.
2. Run a cake scraper (or alternative, see page 37) around the side of the cake to create a flat surface on the buttercream. The side of the cake needs to be straight and at a 90-degree angle to the board. Use a palette knife to smooth out the top surface of the cake; again, this needs to be as flat as possible and make sure the edge of the cake has a good clean line.
3. Put the cake in the fridge for half an hour, until the buttercream has hardened. It is now ready for covering with buttercream, fondant or ganache as described in the following steps.

BUTTERCREAM

The method is the same for buttercream, Swiss meringue buttercream or ganache.

4. Spread a thick layer of the buttercream over the top and sides of the cake with a palette knife (or alternative).
5. Use the palette knife to smooth the buttercream to an even thickness all over the top and side of the cake. The layer should be around 1 cm (⅜ inch) thick.
6. Use a scraper (or plastic ruler) to create a flat surface of buttercream. Place the lower end of the scraper flat against the cake board, with the thin side flush to the buttercream on the side of the cake and run the scraper around the circumference of the cake. You may need to stop at intervals to remove excess buttercream from the scraper. If you can see areas where the scraper has not touched the side, then add some more buttercream with a palette knife. Keep checking that the end of the scraper is on the board. Continue in this manner until the edge of the buttercream is straight.
7. Pull the scraper over the top of the cake and make sure that it is level, either by using a spirit level or by eye. If there are any bumps of buttercream on the edges, flatten them down with a palette knife. You can leave the cake as it is or you can make marks on the buttercream to add texture to the cake. The cake will look more professional if you create a straight edge first and then work the texture on top.

MARZIPAN

When you are rolling out marzipan, always use icing (confectioners') sugar and not cornflour (cornstarch) to sprinkle on the work surface, as cornflour can react with the marzipan.

1. If your cake has a slightly domed top, cut it off with a serrated knife to create a flat surface: measure the sides and mark with cocktail sticks to get a precise flat top.

2. Remove the cocktail sticks and turn the cake upside down. Place it on a board that is at least 5 cm (2 inches) larger than the cake. For example, a 25 cm (10 inch) cake would be placed on an uncovered 30 cm (12 inch) board while you apply the marzipan. Then, when the cake is covered with fondant, you can place it on the covered cake drum. Remember to place the smaller tiers onto the thin cake boards before covering them. Then put the cake (still on the board) on a turntable if you have one, or on a stable flat surface.

3. Brush sugar syrup onto the side of the cake. Roll out a small amount of marzipan into long thin sausages and use these to fill any gaps at the base of the cake. Then use a cake scraper (or ruler) to press against the marzipan sausages and flatten them. This will create a nice flat surface along the side of the cake.

4. Measure the circumference of the cake. Sprinkle the work surface with a fine layer of icing sugar. Roll out half the marzipan into a long strip approximately 5 mm (¼ inch) thick, using spacers if you have them: the length of this strip should be the circumference of the cake. Measure the height of the cake and trim the marzipan strip (along the long edge) until it matches your measurement.

5. Wrap the strip of marzipan around the cake. Use a sharp knife to trim the marzipan where the two ends meet to create a smooth join.

6. Roll out the remaining marzipan into a circular shape to match the top of the cake, again using spacers to create an even thickness, if you have them. Brush the top of the cake with sugar syrup and lay the marzipan circle on top.

7. Trim the edge of the marzipan with a sharp knife.

8. Use two smoothers, or your hands, to smooth down the marzipan. Try to create a sharp edge around the top edge of the cake. Set aside the marzipan-covered cake to stand overnight, so that the marzipan firms up before you add the fondant covering.

MARZIPAN

1

2

3

4

5

6

FONDANT ICING

1. Knead the fondant until it becomes more pliable, but be careful not to overwork it, as this can make it prone to tearing or cracking once it is on the cake.

   Sprinkle a fine layer of cornflour (cornstarch) onto the work surface—use icing (confectioners') sugar if you are using the fondant over marzipan—and rub a little more onto the rolling pin. Lay the fondant down and pat a small amount of cornflour on top.

   Use spacers as a guide when you roll out the fondant; if you are not using spacers, keep a close eye on the fondant to be sure that you are rolling it out evenly. Keep turning the fondant as you are rolling, to make sure it is not sticking to the work surface.

2. When the fondant has been rolled out to the correct thickness, use a smoother to smooth out the surface until there are no bumps or indentations. If you don't have a smoother use the palm of your hand.

   Slide your hands gently under the sheet of fondant. Carefully lift it onto the cake, positioning it centrally. Gently slide your hands out from beneath the surface.

3. With the palms of your hands, smooth down the top of the cake, ensuring there are no air bubbles trapped underneath. If you do find any bubbles, just lift up the fondant to release them and smooth it down again.

4. Use the palms of your hands to secure the fondant around the top edge of the cake: this is the area most likely to crack and tear, so be very gentle. When you are smoothing this area of the cake, work in an upwards direction (rather than pulling the fondant down over the edge of the cake) to help prevent any tearing. Now smooth down the side of the cake, working your way around the circumference. If there are any folds of the fondant at the bottom of the cake, lift up the skirt of fondant and push it in towards the bottom of the cake, unfolding any pleats as you go. Repeat this all around the edge until you have a smooth surface with no folds.

5. Run a finger around the bottom edge of the cake, pressing very gently on the fondant.

6. Cut away excess fondant using a sharp knife.

7. Remove and discard the excess fondant.

8. With a smoother in each hand, work across the top and side of the cake to create a flat and even finish. Or use the palms of your hands. Don't worry if the finish isn't perfect, as you can cover any flaws with the decorations.

   Run the flat side of a cake scraper (or ruler) around the side of the cake, and use it to keep smoothing the fondant until the bottom edge of the cake is even and there are no cracks and gaps between the fondant and the board. You may find there is still some excess fondant that needs to be cut at this point: if there is, then simply smooth the edge again until you have achieved the required finish. Once the cake is covered and the finish on the fondant is as perfect as you can make it, leave it at room temperature in a dry place to firm up overnight before merging the tiers.

ASSEMBLING TIERS

DOWELS

To support the tiers of the cake you will need to use dowels. Dowels are only used to support the layer above them, so naturally the top tier will not need any, unless you are using a heavy cake topper.

1. Place the bottom tier of the cake on the covered cake drum. Take a cake board or cake tin the same size as the next tier up, and gently press it into the centre of the bottom tier. Take it off carefully and you should be left with a faint impression of the cake board on the fondant. This will be your guide to placing the dowels so that they are hidden under the layer above and do not show.

2. Insert the first dowel into the bottom tier, relatively close to the line—say, about half a centimetre or quarter of an inch—inside the guidelines. Use an edible ink pen (or alternative) to mark the point on the dowel where it emerges from the cake. Take this dowel out, and cut it down to the height you have marked.

3. Use the first dowel as a measure to cut the remaining dowels for this tier to the same size. Insert the dowels into the cake making sure that they are spaced evenly just inside the edge of the guideline.

Number of dowels required for different cake sizes

15 cm (6 inch)	3 dowels
18 cm (7 inch)	4 dowels
20 cm (8 inch)	4 dowels
23 cm (9 inch)	5 dowels
25 cm (10 inch)	5 dowels

MERGING THE TIERS

4. Insert the dowels in the bottom tier. If the cake is covered with buttercream, continue to the next step. If the cake is covered with ganache, first spread a blob of melted ganache on top of the bottom cake before adding the next tier. For fondant-covered cakes, take a small grape-size piece of fondant and quickly run it under water from a tap; then massage the fondant until it becomes sticky. Spread this goo onto the top of the first cake.

5. Gently slide your hands under the board of the next tier and carry it over to the bottom tier (obviously, the closer together that you have the cakes at this point, the less chance you have of dropping it). Carefully lower the second tier onto the one below, making sure that it is as central to the bottom tier as possible. Lean the furthest part of the board onto the bottom tier and slide your hands out. The upper tier should only have a small distance to fall until it settles on the bottom tier. Check that the second cake is placed centrally: if it is off-centre then gently (sooo gently) push it from the side using an even pressure until the position is correct. You may need to smooth over the side you pushed if it has any fingerprints, or add a little buttercream or ganache and then smooth it in.

6. Repeat the dowelling process in the next tier, then add the third tier in the same manner as described above. If you are merging buttercream and ganache-covered cakes then you may need to add a little more icing between the tiers if there are any gaps.

MERGING A TALL, THIN CAKE

There are a couple of projects in this book where the tiers are all the same size. Merge the tiers using basically the same method as above, but with a few differences.

1. Insert the dowels 2 cm (¾ inch) in from the edge of the bottom cake.

2. If the cakes are naked cakes (that is, they have no outer covering) use a board that is 2.5 cm (1 inch) smaller than the cake, so a 20 cm (8 inch) cake would sit on an 18 cm (7 inch) board.

For a cake that is covered with the same buttercream all over, crumb-coat the cakes as described in the method on page 45. Merge the tiers before icing and then coat all the cakes with the thick buttercream covering at the same time.

DOWELS

1

2

3

5

A TALL, THIN CAKE

1

2

CHAPTER THREE

Decorating the cake

A wedding cake should not only taste delicious, it should also be a feast for the eyes. Whether you choose a simple design or something more complicated, now is the time to think about the decoration. This is where the fun part really begins!

FONDANT DECORATIONS

In this book I have tried to steer clear of decorations that need advanced sugarcraft skills. Even though I run a cake-decorating business, I have no formal training and I don't practise my art using traditional skills. When I have dabbled with piping or sugar flowers I've learned firsthand how difficult it can be to manipulate fondant or icing into something beautiful. So for the projects in this book I have used techniques that are easy for a beginner to master; however, if you are an expert cake decorator then you may certainly use your skills to add to my designs.

Some of the decorations, such as the cut-out sugar-paste flowers and the roses, can be made well in advance and once they have dried out they can be stored in a cardboard box (never store fondant in an airtight container, as it can sweat and flop). These decorations need to be stored at room temperature and, if you have a packet of silica gel such as you may find inside a new handbag, then put that in the box and it will absorb any excess moisture. To make these decorations you will need a special type of sugar paste called modelling paste (or Mexican paste); don't use florists' paste (gum paste or floral paste) as this has a different consistency and is much more difficult to use. You can buy modelling paste from specialist sugarcraft shops, online or even in some large craft supplies shops, or you can make your own.

EQUIPMENT

Foam mat: you use this to shape sugar flowers with a ball tool. I have done some experimenting and two or three clean kitchen cloths (such as jay cloths, or an equivalent cloth with no texture) on top of each other will work equally well; just make sure they are brand new.

Ball tool: this is a modelling tool. It is a stick with a ball, normally one at each end. There are many uses for it, but for the purposes of this book you will use it to form flowers. You can use your finger, although the shaping will not be as good. You can also use clay-craft ball tools.

Edible food colours: there are many different varieties of edible food colour that you can find in supermarkets or specialist cake-decorating shops, all of which should work equally well in these projects. I would suggest that you test the colours first before you make the actual cake. For instance, I have tested many different edible gold paint colours and some of them need a few layers to achieve the required tone, but for the projects in this book that type of paint would not be suitable, as you need one that has a strong colour and depth of tone. Add the colour into the fondant (or buttercream) with a cocktail stick (toothpick) a little at a time. Knead the colour into the fondant until it is totally incorporated and there are no streaks. It is very easy to add too much colour, as the products nowadays are very intense.

Edible glue: this is used for gluing fondant decorations together or onto the cake. You can buy it online or from cake-decorating suppliers or you can make your own: sprinkle ¼ teaspoon gum tragacanth or CMC powder over 50 ml (1¾ fl oz) water and leave for 10 minutes until it has turned into a gel, then stir with a paintbrush.

Edible ink pens: there are many food-colouring pens on the market and some can be quite weak in colour, so do test them before you start on the final project.

Edible gold spray: I'm sorry to keep repeating myself, but again these sprays can have very different finishes, from a rich gold to a thin glitter. Test and experiment with different brands until you find the most suitable. Also double-check that the spray you are using is edible.

Flower and leaf cutters: you can find these petal and leaf-shape cutter sets in sugarcraft shops or craft supply stores. The easiest to use are the cutters with an incorporated plunger, which makes it easier to release the fondant shape.

PAPER DECORATIONS

It's as easy as pie (or cake) to make fabulous paper toppers to adorn your cake; little bunting flags or signs are especially adorable. Or transform a humble sheet of A4 into a bunch of blooming gorgeous flowers: personally I think that these are the perfect decorations for a handmade wedding cake. You don't need to be a ninja crafter or own hordes of specialist equipment to create paper decorations and they can be made a long time in advance. Store them in a cardboard box to keep them from getting dusty.

You can use tissue or crepe paper for a delicate finish or use scrapbooking paper to add pattern to your design. You can even use coffee filters, either in their natural plain white state or dyed with edible food colour. If you are placing paper flowers onto a buttercream-covered cake then you may need to paint some PVA (craft) glue as a sealer on the underside of the flowers to prevent them from becoming greasy, especially if the temperature is going to be high. You can easily change the colour and style of the flowers to suit the theme of your day. Seek

out unusual colours or patterns as this will only add more interest to the overall design.

Wafer paper (rice paper, confectioners' wafer)—thin edible sheets made from not only rice starch but, surprisingly, from potato starch too—can be used with various techniques to add decoration to a cake. You can print or paint onto these sheets using edible food colours; they can be cut into various shapes or they can be sculpted into gorgeous flowers. You could substitute real paper for the wafer paper projects in this book if you prefer; however the rice paper has a beautiful translucent quality and there is the added bonus that it is totally edible. There are different grades (weights) of rice paper but all should be suitable for these projects and you can get coloured rice paper too, although the range is very limited. Rice paper decorations can be made in advance and stored in a moisture-free environment (any moisture will degrade the paper).

EQUIPMENT

Scalpel or craft knife: this is great for creating intricate shapes, but you can use scissors if you don't own a scalpel.

Scissors: for the paper projects in this book you will need to use good strong and sharp scissors.

Paintbrushes: for creating washes of colour or you can use a soft cake-decorating brush.

Glue gun: these are relatively inexpensive, so if you were intent on a project such as the piñata I would definitely advise you to invest in one: it will make the job so much easier. A hot or cold glue gun would work equally well, but if you really didn't want to buy one then a glue stick or PVA glue will also work.

Wire: florists' wire will work perfectly well for any project that requires wire. The higher the gauge number, the thinner the wire. Always use a lacquered wire in cakes, as uncovered wire is finished with a chemical.

Florists' tape: you can buy this in a variety of colours, so check the specific requirements for each project.

Craft punches: you can buy these in a variety of shapes and sizes from craft shops or online stores.

FRESH FLOWERS

I know that this may sound obvious, but you must make sure that any flower you use on a cake is not poisonous! While the petals of some flowers may be perfectly fine, their leaves or sap may be poisonous, so check with your florist. If you are using your own flowers, research thoroughly to make sure everything you use is harmless.

Try to find pesticide-free organic flowers. Cut flowers are not meant to be an edible product and therefore the pesticide used may be harmful; however, it can be quite difficult to source organic flowers (unless you grow them yourself). I recommend that you thoroughly wash and soak the petals and make sure they are well dried before use.

If you are sticking flowers into a cake it is best to take off the stems and wire the flowers. This stops any dirt, sap or thorns getting into the cake and makes it easier to handle. Wiring helps to anchor the flowers to the cake, prevents heavy heads from drooping and enables you to position the flower at any angle. A florist will wire the flowers on the day of the wedding—possibly even at the venue—to extend the life of the blooms.

Consider the variety of flower that you will use on your cake. If your budget is large enough then you will be able to buy almost any flower that you wish, but using seasonal flowers will definitely be more cost effective. As long as you store flowers in fresh water in a cool area then you will be able to keep them fresh for a few days before the wedding.

If you wish to create a small arrangement of flowers to stand on top of your cake rather than wiring them in, you can use a mini oasis, which will have a small saucer underneath to prevent any moisture being transferred to the cake. This will also extend the life of the flowers. You can source these online or from your local florist. You could also use small bud vases, which you should be able to buy from your local florist, or even use a pretty teacup as a vase.

HOW TO WIRE A FLOWER

1. Cut the stem off the flower as close as possible to the base of the flower head.
2. Push a wire through the base of the flower. Bend the wire in half with the flower in the centre and twist the two ends of the wire together.
3. Cover the wire with florists' tape. This is called a single mount and is suitable for smaller flowers.
4. For a larger flower head you may need a double mount. You wire the flower head in the same manner as before and then add another wire at a 90 degree angle to the first one. Then twist all the wires together and cover them with florists' tape.

EDIBLE FLOWERS

Many flowers in your garden are edible; however, that doesn't mean you should use them on a cake. Some have a bitter taste or a pungent odour. Never use a flower that has been sprayed with chemicals. Double-check anything you use before you eat it and if you are in doubt over a particular bloom, don't use it. You can find lists of edible flowers online. Many supermarkets sell edible flowers in their salad section and there are also online suppliers who can ship you boxes of fresh flowers. You can also use crystallised flowers; again, if you don't want to make your own there are many online suppliers who offer this service. If you are getting married in the middle of the summer or in a particularly warm part of the world then I would advise you to use crystallised flowers. Small and delicate flowers will wilt and the petals will curl up within a couple of hours if they are not in water.

FRUIT

Choose fruit that doesn't have any blemishes. Soft fruit such as strawberries or raspberries should not be overripe, as they can turn mouldy in the time it takes to say 'I do!'

CAKE TOPPERS

I have made quite a few wedding cakes where the couples have made their own cake topper, and I think that this is a really personal touch to the cake. If you are particularly crafty you can make modelling clay figures. There are many companies who specialise in unique wedding cake toppers. If the topper you have chosen is quite heavy then insert a dowel into the top tier of the cake underneath the topper.

CHAPTER FOUR

Kitchen to venue

*I would imagine that very few of you will be holding your wedding ceremony
at home, so you do need to give some thought to the way you will transport the cake.
The temperature and humidity of the day can have an effect on the cake, too,
so do take some time to consider your options.*

STORING THE CAKE

Different cakes will require different methods of storage
and each project will offer advice as to how to store that
particular cake, but here are some general rules.

Fondant-covered cakes should be stored at room
temperature and never in a fridge. If the fondant gets very
cold it will start to sweat as it heats up and this will damage
any decoration you may have created. In the same vein,
never store a fondant-covered cake in an airtight tin as,
again, the fondant will begin to sweat. I usually keep the
cakes I make on a counter until they are required; however,
if you are nervous about leaving your cake out where it
might get damaged, store it in a cardboard box and either
leave the lid off until you need to transport the box or prop
it open a little to create a flow of air.

Cakes covered in Swiss meringue buttercream, ganache
or conventional buttercream will also be best stored at room
temperature; however, if you live in a very hot climate or are
making your cake during a particularly hot spell then these
cakes can be refrigerated.

TRANSPORTING THE CAKE

I would always advise transporting a cake in a box for a
couple of reasons: the first being that when you are carrying
the cake you are not tempted to lean it against your body
and crush or mark any decoration; the second being that if
the cake slides about in the car it won't get dented and if
anything should fall onto it the cake will remain intact.

You can buy wedding cake boxes from many sugarcraft
suppliers; however, these can be expensive. It is much easier
to make your own from a cardboard box. Start by working
out the dimensions of your finished cake. Each tier of your
cake will be roughly 7.5–10 cm (3–4 inches) tall. So for
a three-tier cake I would estimate that it will be roughly
30 cm (12 inches) tall, plus another 2.5 cm (1 inch) to
account for the boards: so you need a box that is 33 cm
(13 inches) tall. For the base of the box you need to create
a snug fit: a 25 cm (10 inch) cake will be on a 30 cm
(12 inch) board, so a box with a base of no more than 33 cm
(13 inches) would be perfect. If you can only source a larger
box don't be too concerned.

The easiest way to get the cake into the box is to cut down
each side, fold each flap down and then, once the cake is in
place, unfold the sides and tape them securely together.
Alternatively you can place the box on its side and slide the
cake in, making sure to secure the flaps before you move

the cake. A square of nonslip mat (you will find this in a hardware or homewares store) placed under the cake will prevent the cake from slipping inside the box.

When carrying a cake, always hold the cake with your hands under the board. The cakes can be very heavy and you need a good grip. Make sure that the cake is held in a level position at all times: if you lean it forward or backwards it may slide or the tiers may crack and bulge.

In the car, where possible, always transport the cake in the boot of the car as this is the flattest part. If necessary, a footwell will be adequate. Never transport a cake on a car seat as these are angled and the cake may crack. Use a square of nonslip mat under the box to prevent the box from moving about during transit. If you do not have any room in the boot or footwell then the cake can be carried on a person's knee (just not the driver's)! The person has the job of ensuring that the cake is flat and not at any angle.

Do not leave a cake in a car overnight as it can affect the covering, and be aware of the temperature in the car. Extreme heat or cold may affect the covering also. Make sure that a ganache or buttercream-covered cake is not sitting with strong sunlight pounding down on it, as it may melt, so if you can, turn the aircon to the highest setting. Drive carefully over any bumps and don't take corners too fast!

DISPLAYING THE CAKE

Many venues will be able to supply a cake stand, but do check it out first as they can often be very large and old fashioned and may not suit the cake you have in mind.

Some of the couples I work with buy their own cake stands to keep as a memento of their big day, and you can easily find beautiful stands to match any theme. Most homewares shops will stock them and many big supermarkets also sell cake stands. If you are looking for something a little different then you may need to look online. There are also many businesses that will hire out vintage crockery, and most of these will be able to supply you with cake stands.

You do not need a cake stand that is bigger than the cake (or the board it is sitting on). A 30 cm (12 inch) board on top of a 25 cm (10 inch) stand will look perfectly fine as long as the cake stand top is flat. There shouldn't be too much discrepancy in the sizes of the cake and cake stand to prevent any wobbling.

You can opt for a more unusual cake stand if you prefer. A cut log will make a great display for a rustic cake, but do make sure that the cake is on a board to prevent any contamination. An upside-down teacup with a large plate glued to the top of it will be perfect for a vintage-style cake, or you could use a vase filled with flowers for a more stylish look. Just make sure that the cake is sitting firm on top of the stand or the cutting of the cake may end up as a viral video! You could even cover a box or a tin with fabric or paper to match your cake. Use your imagination to create something fabulous.

You will find advice in each project in this book to help you with your timings: when to set your cake up for display, how long it will take you. Do bear these in mind when you are considering which cake to make.

STYLING AND PROPS

You may wish to add extra decoration to the background of the cake, especially if the cake is in front of an area that doesn't suit the theme. If you are at a venue where you cannot attach anything to the wall, consider using a screen. You can make or buy pompoms, honeycomb balls, balloons or bunting. You could even create your own backdrop from paper flowers. Try to use a tablecloth that will complement the cake you have made.

CUTTING THE CAKE

If you want to take the traditional 'cutting of the cake' photograph then don't forget to leave an ornamental knife when you are setting up the cake. Most venues will be able to supply you with one, but if you have organised your own location you will need to supply your own. As a very special keepsake of the day you could have your initials and the date of your wedding engraved into the knife.

All of the projects in this book include portion numbers for each tier of the cake. When you are ready to cut the cake, remove each tier (where applicable) by sliding a knife under its board and lifting it off. Set the tier on a flat surface: don't cut the cake while it is still on top of another tier.

1. To cut the cakes in such a way as to produce clean sharp cuts and portions of equal sizes, use a large serrated knife or a long knife with a thin blade. Wipe the blade with a warm, damp cloth every few cuts to prevent any drag on the cake or smearing.

2. Cut each cake into portions using the diagram shown below as a guide.

3. Remove the dowels as you cut the cake.

If you are getting married at a venue with staff that will cut and serve the cake for you, make sure you inform the caterer how many dowels need to be removed before serving and if there any other non-edible items on the cake.

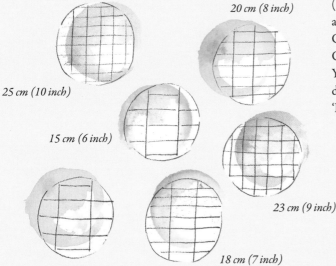

20 cm (8 inch)

25 cm (10 inch)

15 cm (6 inch)

23 cm (9 inch)

12.5 cm (5 inch)

18 cm (7 inch)

PROJECTS

Throughout this book I have included timings with each recipe to give you an indication of the maximum time that particular cake will take; however, do remember that these timings are based on just one person doing all the work. While some timings will not change if you have help, others can be drastically reduced; for example, making the decoration for the 'Chocolate Boom!' project will take one person 7½ hours, but gather together seven of your friends and you could make all the flowers in less than an hour.

I would recommend that you test a recipe long before you make it as your wedding cake. There is no need to make a whole stacked cake, or even a whole tier: where possible, you could make just one layer of the cake. You should definitely check that you both like the flavour of the particular cake you have chosen.

The most important aspect of your wedding cake is that it suits your taste, both literally and aesthetically. I have created recipes and decorations in these projects that I feel fit together well; however, you can customise all of these projects for yourself. Mix up the flavour combinations from three different projects with the decorations from another.

Tiered cakes will appear in proportion if there is about a difference of 5 cm (2 inches) between each tier; that is, a 25 cm (10 inch), 20 cm (8 inch) and 15 cm (6 inch) cake will always be visually pleasing. So, for example, if you were to create your own combination you could bake a 25 cm (10 inch) fruit cake from the 'Infinite Love' project, add a 20 cm (8 inch) salted caramel cake from the 'Sparkling Celebration' project and a 15 cm (6 inch) strawberry and Champagne cake from the 'Watercolour Sunset' project. You could then cover all these cakes with fondant and decorate them with the fabric collars and bunting from the 'Bee's Knees' project. You really can cake it your own way!

part two

THE
PROJECTS

CHAPTER ONE

Romantic beginnings

The Oxford dictionary defines romance as 'a feeling of excitement and mystery associated with love', which I have always thought a rather lovely definition, and which probably correctly describes the emotions that most couples experience at the beginning of their courtship (yes, courtship: no apologies for using that old-fashioned word, it's one of my all-time favourites). If any day calls for a big gesture then perhaps this is it: and the archetypal romantic couple in this vein would have to be Romeo and Juliet, the star-crossed lovers, who made the biggest gesture of all, risking all for their love. The projects in this chapter are ideal for starry-eyed lovers: they combine traditional flavours with romantic styling, and could be a perfect way to express your love for your very own Romeo or Juliet. Let's say that Shakespeare got the ending wrong. All that messing about with potions was the problem: they'd have been all right if they'd just stuck to cake.

THE CAKES

Infinite Love

RICH FRUIT CAKE

This design is inspired by eternal love: decorated with a repeated flower shape, a pure white bloom symbolising the love that will surround the couple's new life together.

Underneath the layer of flowers the cake is a traditional fruit cake (the recipe has been handed down in my family through many generations), and as you cut into the cake you will see the plump raisins and sultanas representing all the fruits and blessings that will grow during married life together... and it tastes amazing!

Do feel free to alter the mixture of fruit used in the cake to cater for your own tastes: dried tropical fruit, blueberries, cranberries or even nuts would be delicious, and you can change the spices too, in order to complement any different ingredients. If you dislike marzipan, or are allergic to it, then cover the cake with two layers of fondant instead, leaving the first layer to dry overnight before adding the next.

'INFINITE LOVE' AT A GLANCE

BAKING SKILL: MEDIUM

Making sure that a fruit cake is baked evenly without it drying out or being undercooked can be a test of nerves and does require some baking experience; however, if you are worried that it may be overcooked simply baste it with more brandy to increase the moistness.

DECORATING SKILL: EASY

HOW FAR IN ADVANCE CAN IT BE MADE?

Fruit cake is best made at least three months in advance of the wedding day. This gives time for the flavours to develop and mature, and you can 'feed' the cake with liquor to create a rich, deep flavour. But don't discount this cake if you are organising a last-minute wedding, or a last-minute cake: even if it is baked just a few days in advance, it will still taste amazing. The cake can be covered and decorated up to two weeks before required and stored in a cardboard box.

SETTING UP:

Takes around five minutes. The cake is already tiered and decorated so it is just a matter of placing the finished cake on the table or cake stand. Set up from 24 hours before required. High humidity may affect the paste flowers.

PORTIONS:

15 cm (6 inch) tier, 12 portions;
20 cm (8 inch) tier, 28 portions;
25 cm (10 inch) tier, 48 portions.

PRICE PER PORTION: LOW

TOTAL MAKING TIME:

13–21½ hours (depending on how you bake the cakes).

ON THE DAY:

You may find it helpful to take a few extra flowers with you when you set up in case there are any breakages.

FRUIT CAKE

PREP: 24 hours before baking, 10 minutes; baking day, 30 minutes per cake

- -

15 CM (6 INCH) CAKE: bake for 3–3½ hours

300 g (10½ oz) currants
150 g (5½ oz) sultanas (golden raisins)
100 g (3½ oz) raisins
75 g (2¾ oz) mixed peel (mixed candied citrus peel)
75 g (2¾ oz) glacé cherries
30 ml (1 fl oz) brandy (or other alcohol), or use orange juice
150 g (5½ oz) plain (all-purpose) flour
1 teaspoon ground ginger
1 teaspoon ground cinnamon
1 teaspoon mixed (pumpkin pie) spice
¼ teaspoon freshly grated nutmeg
pinch of salt
150 g (5½ oz) unsalted butter
150 g (5½ oz) dark brown sugar
3 eggs
grated zest of 1 orange and 1 lemon

20 CM (8 INCH) CAKE: bake for 4–4½ hours

500 g (1 lb 2 oz) currants
225 g (8 oz) sultanas (golden raisins)
125 g (4½ oz) raisins
125 g (4½ oz) mixed peel (mixed candied citrus peel)
125 g (4½ oz) glacé cherries
40 ml (1¼ fl oz) brandy (or other alcohol), or use orange juice
225 g (8 oz) plain (all-purpose) flour
1 teaspoon ground ginger
1 teaspoon ground cinnamon
1 teaspoon mixed (pumpkin pie) spice
½ teaspoon freshly grated nutmeg
pinch of salt
225 g (8 oz) unsalted butter
225 g (8 oz) dark brown sugar
4 eggs
grated zest of 1 orange and 1 lemon

25 CM (10 INCH) CAKE: bake for 5–5½ hours

1 kg (2 lb 4 oz) currants
450 g (1 lb) sultanas (golden raisins)
250 g (9 oz) raisins
250 g (9 oz) mixed peel (mixed candied citrus peel)
250 g (9 oz) glacé cherries
80 ml (2½ fl oz/⅓ cup) brandy (or other alcohol),
*   or you can use orange juice*
450 g (1 lb) plain (all-purpose) flour
2 teaspoons ground ginger
2 teaspoons ground cinnamon
2 teaspoons mixed (pumpkin pie) spice
½ teaspoon freshly grated nutmeg
large pinch of salt
450 g (1 lb) unsalted butter
450 g (1 lb) dark brown sugar
8 eggs
grated zest of 2 oranges and 2 lemons

brandy or sugar syrup (see page 34), for basting the cakes
*   during storage*

METHOD

1. Twenty-four hours before you wish to bake the cakes, put all the dried fruit in a large bowl (if you are baking all three cakes at once, use three separate bowls to avoid any confusion with weights). Pour boiling water over the fruit—enough to cover it all completely—as this will really plump up the fruit and help it to absorb the alcohol or fruit juice. Soak for 10 minutes, then drain off all the water. Add the brandy (or fruit juice if you do not want to use alcohol) to the now-plump fruit, mix well, cover the bowl and stand overnight.

2. The next day, preheat the oven to 150°C (300°F).

3. Grease the cake tin(s) with butter, then line with a double layer of baking paper.

4. Sift the flour, spices and salt together into a bowl.

5. Beat the butter and sugar together until the mixture has lightened in colour and takes on a more fluffy appearance: this should take at least 5 minutes.

6. Break the eggs into a bowl and then add them little by little into the cake mixture, while you beat constantly. If the cake batter starts to separate and looks like it has curdled, add a small amount of the flour mixture until it doesn't look curdled anymore. Do not be concerned if this happens, as the cake will still be amazing!

7. Using a large spoon, fold in the flour mixture.

8. Add the orange and lemon zest and mix until well combined.

9. Add the soaked fruit and gently fold through the mixture until well combined.

10. Transfer the mixture to the cake tin and cover the top of the cake with a circle of baking paper (make it slightly larger than the circumference of the tin: this is to protect the top of the cake and prevent the fruit from scorching).

11. Bake for the specified time for the size of the cake. The cake is ready when the surface is a rich golden brown and a skewer inserted into the middle of the cake comes out clean.

12. Once the cake has finished baking, remove it from the oven and immediately prick its surface all over using a cocktail stick (toothpick). Then baste the cake with 4 teaspoons of brandy or sugar syrup (see page 34).

13. Leave the cake to cool in its tin for 30 minutes, then turn out onto a wire rack to cool completely.

14. Once the cake has completely cooled, wrap it in baking paper and then either foil or plastic wrap and store it in an airtight container.

15. Every few weeks, unwrap the cake and baste it with brandy, then re-cover and return the cake to the container to mature.

COVERING THE CAKE

PREP: 24 hours ahead, covering the drum, 10 minutes; then 30–40 minutes per tier plus 12 hours drying time for the marzipan.

EQUIPMENT
rolling pin
spacers (optional)
smoothers (optional)
sharp knife
30 cm (12 inch) covered cake drum (see page 41)
30 cm (12 inch) cake board
25 cm (10 inch) cake board
two 20 cm (8 inch) thin cake boards
15 cm (6 inch) thin cake board

MARZIPAN
15 cm (6 inch): 600 g (1 lb 5 oz)
20 cm (8 inch): 1 kg (2 lb 4 oz)
25 cm (10 inch): 1.45 kg (3 lb 3½ oz)

FONDANT
15 cm (6 inch): 600 g (1 lb 5 oz)
20 cm (8 inch): 800 g (1 lb 12 oz)
25 cm (10 inch): 1.25 kg (2 lb 12 oz)
500 ml (17 fl oz/2 cups) sugar syrup (you can make the syrup using the alcohol with which you have chosen to flavour the cake if you prefer: simply substitute it for the water in the recipe on page 34)

1. Cover the cakes with marzipan using the method described on page 46.

   When covering the 25 cm (10 inch) cake, stand it on the 30 cm (12 inch) cake board. Once the cake has been covered with the fondant you can transfer it to the covered cake drum. Stand the smaller cakes on the thin cake boards before covering them.

2. Leave the marzipan to harden for a day, then slightly dampen the surface with water and cover the cakes with fondant using the method described on page 49.

ASSEMBLING THE TIERS

PREP: 20 minutes

Dowel and assemble the tiers using the method described on page 50.

DECORATING THE CAKE

*PREP: modelling paste,10 minutes plus 12 hours resting; royal icing, 10 minutes;
cutting out and attaching the flowers, 4 hours*

EQUIPMENT

flower cutter, such as a 3 cm (1¼ inch) daisy cutter
foam mat (for alternatives, see page 53)
rolling pin
cornflour (cornstarch)
ball tool (if you are happy with chunkier
   flowers, this is optional)
foil
paintbrush or cocktail stick (toothpick)
500 g (1 lb 2 oz) modelling paste (see below for recipe,
   or use ready-made modelling paste)

MODELLING PASTE

500 g (1 lb 2 oz) fondant
2 teaspoons gum tragacanth (CMC or Tylose)

ROYAL ICING

100 g (3½ oz) icing (confectioners') sugar
3 g (⅛ oz) meri-white powder
10–15 ml (⅜–½ fl oz) water

1. Make the modelling paste using the method on page 34. (If you are using gum tragacanth you need to do this 24 hours before you need the paste.) Combine the ingredients for the royal icing or use 50 ml (1¾ fl oz) of edible glue (see page 54).

2. Begin by cutting the foil into 4 cm (1½ inch) square pieces. Pinch one side of the square together to form a slight cone shape. These will help to shape the flowers. There is no need to cut out a foil square for each flower, because you can place the flowers on the cake as soon as they are dry and reuse the foil. I would suggest starting by making 50.

3. Sprinkle the work surface with a fine layer of cornflour. Take a walnut-size piece of the modelling paste and roll it out to a thickness of 1 mm (1⁄32 inch). Make sure that the rest of the modelling paste is covered with plastic wrap or stored in a resealable plastic bag, as it can dry out very quickly.

4. Cut out as many flowers as possible from the rolled out paste and place them on the foam mat.

5. Gently roll the ball tool over the petals to thin them out, but don't press too hard or you will tear them.

6. Make a small circular motion in the middle of the flower, pressing gently. This action should make the petals lift slightly, giving a three-dimensional effect. Place the flower into a cone of foil and set aside to dry. You will need roughly 300 flowers to cover all three tiers, and a minimum of 20 extras to allow for breakages.

7. The flowers should be dried out enough to attach to the cake after about 30 minutes.

8. If you are gluing the flowers to the cake fairly soon after making them then edible glue will be sufficient. Brush the middle of the back of each flower with the glue and attach it to the cake, then press the centre of the flower gently to firm it down. However, if you have made the flowers in advance and they are completely dry, using royal icing instead of glue will make it easier to attach them. Use a cocktail stick to add a small blob of icing to the back of each flower then attach them to the cake using the same method as described for the glue.

9. Start at the bottom of the cake and glue a row of flowers in place as described in step 8.

10. When you start to add the next row of flowers, offset them so that their centres are in line with the gaps in the row below.

11. Continue placing flowers in this manner until the cake is covered.

12. If any flowers break during transport, simply remove the broken flowers and repeat step 8 to attach the spare flowers that you made in step 6.

SHAPING & APPLYING FLOWERS 6

12

Amore Neapolitan

CHOCOLATE, RASPBERRY
AND VANILLA CAKES

Do you remember eating neapolitan ice cream when you were a child? It is typical of the desserts that were served up by my granny (along with a delicious homemade trifle).

Sometimes a wedding is a great excuse to return to childhood memories: I have been to very few where the guests passed up the chance to do the Hokey-Pokey. I have created a modern, romantic version of the traditional neapolitan ice cream in cake form, although—possibly controversially—I have substituted raspberries for strawberries in the middle layer. And while the flavours do hark back to childhood days, the cake has a more grown-up sophisticated style to please all your guests, young and old.

'AMORE NEAPOLITAN' AT A GLANCE

BAKING SKILL: EASY

Although each cake is a different flavour, they are all versions of a classic sponge cake recipe.

DECORATING SKILL: EASY

The buttercream frosting is very easy to apply and the flowers will cover any flaws.

HOW FAR IN ADVANCE CAN IT BE MADE?

The cake layers can be baked up to five days before the wedding; filled, covered and the tiers assembled up to four days before the big day. Add the flowers on the day itself. Alternatively, the cake layers can be made up to three months in advance of the day and frozen. Leave them at room temperature to defrost completely before filling with the buttercream. The buttercream can also be made up to three months in advance and frozen in airtight containers. Leave to defrost for 12 hours in a fridge before use: you will probably have to beat it, to make it soft enough to use.

SETTING UP:

This shouldn't take any more than half an hour to set up, if all the flowers are wired in advance.

The flowers will keep their shape for 6–10 hours, depending on the room temperature and how far in advance they are wired. The cake, without the flowers, will be perfect all day, or it can even be set up the night before; however, if the celebration is in a very hot venue (or if the cake is in front of a very sunny window) the buttercream may melt.

PORTIONS:

15 cm (6 inch) tier, 12 portions;
20 cm (8 inch) tier, 28 portions;
25 cm (10 inch) tier, 46 portions.

PRICE PER PORTION: LOW

TOTAL MAKING TIME:

5½ hours plus 1½ hours chilling time.

TOTAL BAKING TIME:

Up to 4 hours if baking each layer individually or 1¾ hours if baking three layers at once.

CAKE RECIPES

PREP: 20 minutes per layer. Because each tier of this cake is a different flavour you will not be able to bake a layer of each of the tiers at the same time; however, if you can beg, steal or borrow three cake tins of the same size you can bake all three layers of each tier at once, which will shorten the baking time. Ingredients quantities are for each layer; you will need three layers for each tier.

---

15 CM (6 INCH) VANILLA BEAN CAKE LAYER

50 g (1¾ oz) butter
50 g (1¾ oz) sugar
1 egg
1 vanilla bean, seeds scraped, or ½ teaspoon vanilla bean paste
50 g (1¾ oz) self-raising flour
1 tablespoon milk

20 CM (8 INCH) RASPBERRY CAKE LAYER

100 g (3½ oz) raspberries
130 g (4½ oz) sugar
100 g (3½ oz) butter
finely grated zest of 1 lemon
2 eggs
100 g (3½ oz) self-raising flour
1 tablespoon lemon juice

25 CM (10 INCH) CHOCOLATE CAKE LAYER

175 g (6 oz) butter
175 g (6 oz) light brown sugar
3 eggs
1 teaspoon vanilla extract
¼ teaspoon coffee extract
130 g (4½ oz) self-raising flour
45 g (1½ oz) unsweetened cocoa powder
4 tablespoons milk

1. Preheat the oven to 190°C (375°F). Lightly grease and line the cake tin(s) with baking paper.

2. For the raspberry cake, put the raspberries and 30 g (1 oz) of the sugar in a saucepan over very low heat. Stir the raspberries vigorously until they start to break down. Once they have released their juice and the sugar has dissolved increase the heat to medium and simmer for 8–10 minutes until the mixture has thickened. Remove from the heat. Pass the raspberries through a sieve to remove all the seeds. You will need to push the fruit through the sieve with a metal spoon to extract as much fruit pulp as possible. There should only be seeds remaining in the sieve. Leave the purée to cool.

3. Beat the butter and sugar (and the lemon zest, when making the raspberry cake) together for at least 5 minutes. The mixture should become noticeably paler and take on a fluffy appearance.

4. Add the eggs one at a time and beat them in well. If the mixture starts to curdle, add a spoonful of the flour and beat again. If making the vanilla cake, add the vanilla seeds or paste now. If making the chocolate cake, add the vanilla and coffee extracts now.

5. Sift the flour (and the cocoa powder, if making the chocolate cake) into the mixture. Use a large metal spoon to gently fold in the flour.

6. Fold in the milk and mix until well combined. If you are making the raspberry cake, fold in the lemon juice and raspberry purée.

7. Spoon the batter into the cake tin(s). Bake for 25–30 minutes. The cake is ready when a cake tester or skewer inserted into the centre of the cake comes out clean.

8. Allow the cake to cool in the tin for 10 minutes and then turn out onto a wire rack to cool completely.

BUTTERCREAM

PREP: 10 minutes per batch; however, if you are using a hand whisk you may need to make the chocolate buttercream in two batches, so it will take a little longer.

VANILLA BUTTERCREAM
350 g (12 oz) unsalted butter
350 g (12 oz) icing (confectioners') sugar (or unrefined icing sugar if you don't mind a creamier colour)
1½ teaspoons vanilla bean paste

RASPBERRY BUTTERCREAM
550 g (1 lb 4 oz) unsalted butter
550 g (1 lb 4 oz) icing (confectioners') sugar
finely grated zest of 2 lemons
100 g (3½ oz) raspberries

CHOCOLATE BUTTERCREAM
650 g (1 lb 7 oz) unsalted butter
160 g (5¾ oz) unsweetened cocoa powder
490 g (1 lb 1½ oz) unrefined icing (confectioners') sugar
2 teaspoons vanilla extract (or vanilla bean paste)
½ teaspoon coffee extract

1. Beat the butter with the icing sugar (and cocoa powder, for the chocolate buttercream) until light and fluffy.

2. For the vanilla and chocolate buttercream add the vanilla bean paste (and the coffee extract) and mix well to combine.

3. For the raspberry buttercream, make a raspberry purée to add as flavouring by putting the raspberries in a saucepan over low heat; vigorously stir and bash them about with a wooden spoon until the berries disintegrate and they begin to release their juice. Take the saucepan off the heat and pass the raspberries through a sieve using the method described in step 2 of the cake instructions on page 77. Allow to cool, then beat into the buttercream mixture.

LEVELLING AND FILLING THE LAYERS

PREP: 24 hours ahead, covering the drum, 10 minutes; 10–15 minutes per cake, plus 20–30 minutes chilling time.

EQUIPMENT
30 cm (12 inch) cake board: you will need a board this size to place the largest cake on while it is being layered and filled (this will make it easier to transport around the kitchen)
30 cm (12 inch) covered cake drum (see page 41), optional: you can transport the cake to the venue using the uncovered board, then transfer the cake to a cake stand
25 cm (10 inch) cake board
two 20 cm (8 inch) thin cake boards
15 cm (6 inch) thin cake board
cake leveller, or cocktail sticks (toothpicks) and a serrated knife
small palette knife (I would advise investing in one for this project as it will make it much easier, but you can still achieve a desirable effect with a substitute, see page 37)

Level and fill the cakes using the method described on pages 37 and 42. Each layer of buttercream filling should be around 1 cm (⅜ inch) deep. Remember to place the bottom tiers of the 20 cm (8 inch) and 15 cm (6 inch) cakes on to a thin cake board before you start filling. Then crumb coat each cake (see page 45) and refrigerate for 20–30 minutes, until the buttercream has hardened.

COVERING THE CAKE

PREP: 5–10 minutes per cake

Add a thick layer of the flavoured buttercream to each cake. You will not need to layer as much on the top of the cake as on the sides, as you don't want the frosting to bulge up once you have assembled the tiers, so add just enough to cover the crumb coat and enable you to incorporate some texture. Then spend a little time achieving a balanced texture around the cake using the palette knife.

Keep a few tablespoons of each of the three buttercreams to one side for any touch-ups needed after assembling the tiers, or after setting up the cake.

ASSEMBLING THE TIERS

PREP: 20 minutes

Dowel and assemble the tiers using the method described on page 50. If you have any gaps between the cakes once they are stacked, fill these with some buttercream.

DECORATING THE CAKE

PREP: 40 minutes to wire the flowers, 10 minutes to attach them to the cake

EQUIPMENT
7 large roses
6 medium roses
10 spray roses
7 chrysanthemums
9 sets of leaves
26-gauge florists' wire for the smaller flowers
18-gauge florists' wire for the larger flower heads
florists' tape
wire cutters (although you may get away with a pair of very strong kitchen scissors)

Wire the flowers using the method described on page 57, remembering to completely cover the ends of the stems as this will give the flowers a longer shelf life and prevent any sap seeping into the cake.

Add the flowers to the cake, starting from the top and working down. Add the larger flowers first and then hide any visible wires with leaves or small spray roses. Try not to create a symmetrical design, as asymmetry is more pleasing to the eye. The number of flowers I have recommended for this project will only be enough to decorate the front of the cake, so if you wish to have flowers all around then double the amounts specified.

Nuts About You

HAZELNUT & CHOCOLATE CAKE

The lovely man I married 'for better or worse' (and he would probably say the latter), now lives with a professional cake maker and is forced to sample an awful lot of cake, so much so that he has grown positively weary of baked goods.

Fortunately for me, he rarely complains; however, even with his jaded palette he could not get enough of this particular cake, proclaiming it 'the best ever!' I count that as the highest praise. It would be a particularly suitable cake to serve as a dessert, especially with lashings of whipped cream and berries.

'NUTS ABOUT YOU' AT A GLANCE

BAKING SKILL: HARD

The cake recipe is based on a genoise sponge, which is more complicated to make than a normal sponge cake and does require some baking experience, as does caramelising sugar to make the praline. Also the cake is covered in a Swiss meringue buttercream that, similarly, can be trickier to make. You could always use a more traditional buttercream if you wanted, or even make more of the ganache and cover the cake with that.

I would advise against attempting this recipe if you do not have an electric whisk, unless you are hoping to firm up your arms ready for the big day! Making the buttercream will be so much easier if you have the use of a standing mixer.

DECORATING SKILL: MEDIUM

The buttercream frosting is very easy to apply, but you do have to work for a while to create the nice flat sides. Making the wafer-paper flowers can take a little practice. The trickiest part to working with wafer paper is getting the moisture level right, but if you give yourself plenty of time to experiment with making the flowers beforehand you will be sure to master the technique.

HOW FAR IN ADVANCE CAN IT BE MADE?

You can make the cake layers up to five days before required, or they can be baked and frozen up to three months in advance. The ganache can be made a week in advance and stored in a refrigerator. The praline can be made up to a month in advance and stored in an airtight plastic container. The paper flowers can be made up to a month in advance and stored in an airtight container. The cake can be layered, assembled and covered up to four days in advance, but only add the flowers after you have set it up.

SETTING UP:

This shouldn't take any more than half an hour to set out. The cake will be perfect all day once it has been set up, as long as the room temperature is normal. It can also be set up the day before. Do be aware that if it is in a very hot venue (or if the cakes are in a window) the frosting may start to melt. The flowers will last for days as long as they are kept dry.

PORTIONS:

Each tier will serve 25, so 50 in total for the cake as pictured.

PRICE PER PORTION: HIGH

TOTAL MAKING TIME:

5½ hours plus 2½ hours for cooling and chilling.

TOTAL BAKING TIME:

1 hour 40 minutes.

CAKE RECIPES

PREP: 20 minutes per batch. Ingredients quantities are for two layers of the hazelnut and one layer of the chocolate. To recreate this cake you will need two tiers, each tier containing two layers of hazelnut sponge and one layer of chocolate sponge: a total of four layers of hazelnut, and two layers of chocolate.

- -

HAZELNUT LAYER: bake for 20–25 minutes

100 g (3½ oz) butter

6 eggs

250 g (9 oz) caster (superfine) sugar

200 g (7 oz) plain (all-purpose) flour

50 g (1¾ oz) ground hazelnuts (if this ingredient is hard to find, buy whole or chopped blanched hazelnuts and blitz them in a food processor: don't worry if they form something of a paste, as they will still work perfectly well)

- -

CHOCOLATE LAYER: bake for 20–25 minutes

50 g (1¾ oz) butter

3 eggs

125 g (4½ oz) caster (superfine) sugar

90 g (3¼ oz) plain (all-purpose) flour

35 g (1¼ oz) unsweetened cocoa powder

1. Preheat the oven to 190°C (375°F), lightly grease and line the cake tins with baking paper: you will use two 20 cm (8 inch) cake tins for the hazelnut layers and one 20 cm (8 inch) cake tin for the chocolate layer, for each tier.

2. Melt the butter and set it aside to cool.

3. Fill a large saucepan one-third full with water and bring to the boil.

4. Put the eggs and sugar in a large heatproof bowl that fits snugly into the saucepan without the bottom of the bowl touching the water (the mixture will dramatically increase in size, so do make sure that you are using a large bowl). Once the water has boiled take the saucepan off the heat and set the bowl on the top. Whisk the sugar and eggs together for 10 minutes. The mixture should triple in size and become very pale and fluffy. After 10 minutes it should have reached the 'ribbon stage': if you lift the beaters out of the bowl a ribbon of the mixture should form on the top, this should take 3–4 seconds to disappear back into the batter.

5. When making the hazelnut layers, mix together the flour and ground hazelnuts. When making the chocolate layer, sift the flour and cocoa powder together. For all layers, shake half of the flour mixture over the top of the egg mixture and fold it in very gently using a large slotted spoon or a spatula. You don't want to lose any of the air that you have beaten in to the batter, but you must make sure that all the flour is incorporated. Fold in the remaining flour mixture.

6. Slowly pour the melted butter into the mix and fold it in very gently.

7. For the hazelnut layers, divide the mixture between two prepared tins. For the chocolate layer, pour the mixture into the prepared tin.

8. Bake for 20–25 minutes until the top is firm but springy to the touch and a skewer inserted into the centre comes out clean. Allow to cool in the tin for 5 minutes, then turn out onto a wire rack to cool completely.

PRALINE

PREP: 25 minutes plus half an hour for cooling

- -

300 g (10½ oz) hazelnuts
300 g (10½ oz) refined caster (superfine) sugar

1. Line a baking tray with baking paper and spread the hazelnuts on the tray. You don't want them too spaced out, but also not in a pile.

2. Caramelise the sugar using the method on page 34.

3. Pour the caramelised sugar over the hazelnuts and set aside to cool and harden.

4. Once cooled, break the praline into smaller pieces, put the pieces in a food processor or blender and process until they are the required consistency. You will need a relatively fine powder for the ganache and slightly chunkier breadcrumb-size pieces for decoration.

PRALINE GANACHE

PREP: 10 minutes, plus an hour for cooling.
Ingredients quantities for two tiers.

- -

800 g (1 lb 12 oz) dark chocolate (53% cocoa)
400 ml (14 fl oz) thick (double) cream
200 g (7 oz) hazelnut praline, powdered

1. Make the ganache using the method described on page 34.

2. Add the powdered praline and mix to combine well. Set aside to cool for 1 hour.

SWISS MERINGUE BUTTERCREAM

PREP: 25 minutes, Ingredients quantities for two tiers.

- -

300 g (10½ oz) dark chocolate (70% cocoa)
6 egg whites
400 g (14 oz) refined caster (superfine) sugar
600 g (1 lb 5 oz) unsalted butter, chopped into small pieces,
*   softened*
4 tablespoons hazelnut liqueur

1. Melt the chocolate and set aside to cool slightly.

2. Make the Swiss meringue buttercream using the method described on page 34.

3. Beat in the liqueur and the cooled melted chocolate.

LEVELLING AND FILLING THE LAYERS

*PREP: 24 hours ahead, covering the board, 10 minutes; 10–15 minutes per cake,
then 20–30 minutes chilling time per cake.*

- -

EQUIPMENT
23 cm (9 inch) or 25 cm (10 inch) covered cake drum
two 25 cm (10 inch) cake boards
18 cm (7 inch) thin cake board
cake leveller, or toothpicks and a serrated knife
*small palette knife (I would advise investing in one for this
    project as it will make it much easier, but you can still
    achieve a desirable effect with a substitute, see page 37)*
cake scraper or alternative (see page 37)

Level and fill the cakes using the methods described on
pages 37 and 42. Use the 25 cm (10 inch) uncovered
boards to work on initially, then move the cakes to the
covered drum. Each tier of the cake will consist of two
hazelnut layers with a chocolate layer sandwiched in the
middle. Use a quarter of the praline ganache for each layer
of filling, remember to place one of the tiers on a thin
18 cm (7 inch) cake board before you start filling. Then
crumb coat each cake with the Swiss meringue buttercream,
using the method described on page 45, and refrigerate for
20–30 minutes, until the buttercream has hardened.

ASSEMBLING THE TIERS

PREP: 10–15 minutes

- -

Dowel and assemble the tiers using the method described
on page 50.

COVERING THE CAKE

PREP: 30 minutes

- -

Add a thick layer of the Swiss meringue buttercream to the
tops and the sides of the cakes. Use a tool with a straight
edge to achieve straight sides. (Of course, you can give it
a slight texture if you prefer.)

Cover the outside of the cake with crumbled praline.
Place the cake on a baking tray, form your hand into a scoop
shape, fill the palm with praline and gently press it onto the
cake. You can reapply any praline that falls off.

DECORATING THE CAKE

CRAFT TIME: 2 hours

EQUIPMENT

10 sheets of wafer paper
scissors
templates (page 228)
cocktail sticks (toothpicks)
a container of water

To create this cake you will need one rose of each size: small, medium and large. Start with the large rose.

1. Cut out 2 each of templates A, B, and C, 3 of template D and 1 of E. I wouldn't advise you to trace around the templates on the paper, as you will see the pencil mark on the finished rose, and it won't matter if your cutting out isn't perfect: the final petal will still look gorgeous. Make slits in the petals as indicated on the templates.

2. Take one of the size A petal cutouts. Wet your forefinger in the water, shake off any excess drops, then rub your finger and thumb together so that they are both just damp, rather than wet. Moisten the edge of each petal in a strip about 1 cm (⅜ inch) wide by rubbing it between your finger and thumb. Moisten the centre in the same way and then just hold it in your hands for a few seconds: don't put it down or it may stick to the surface. Once you can feel the areas you have moistened start to soften then you can begin to form the rose shape.

3. The next part is a little fiddly, but gets easier with practice. Curl each alternate petal up towards the middle of the flower and stick the edges together: they should overlap each other by about half.

4. If the petals are not damp enough to stick to each other, dab a little more moisture onto the area you need to stick. Be cautious though, as too much moisture will cause the wafer paper to melt.

5. Then take each of the remaining unstuck petals, and curl those towards the centre in the same way, sticking them to each other and to the petals already »

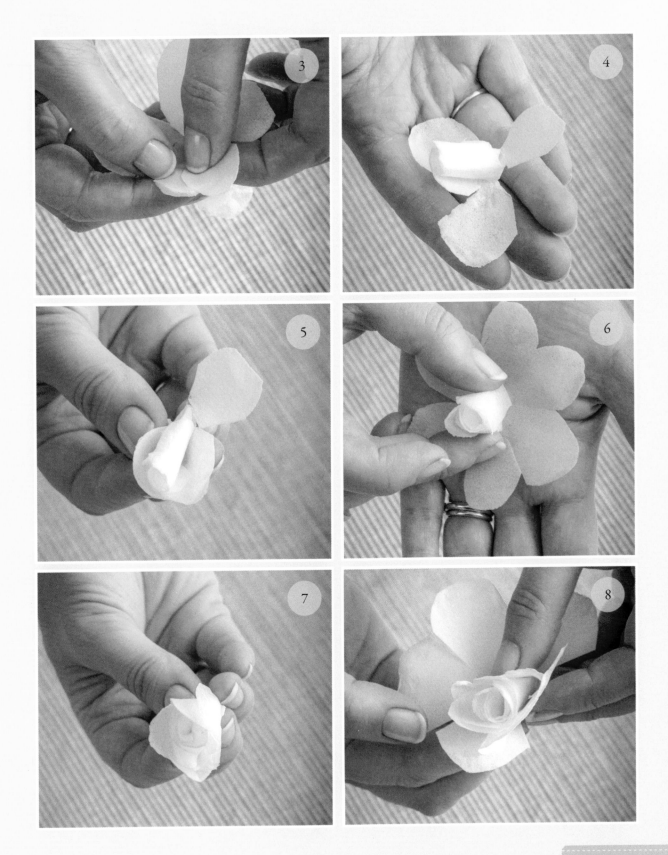

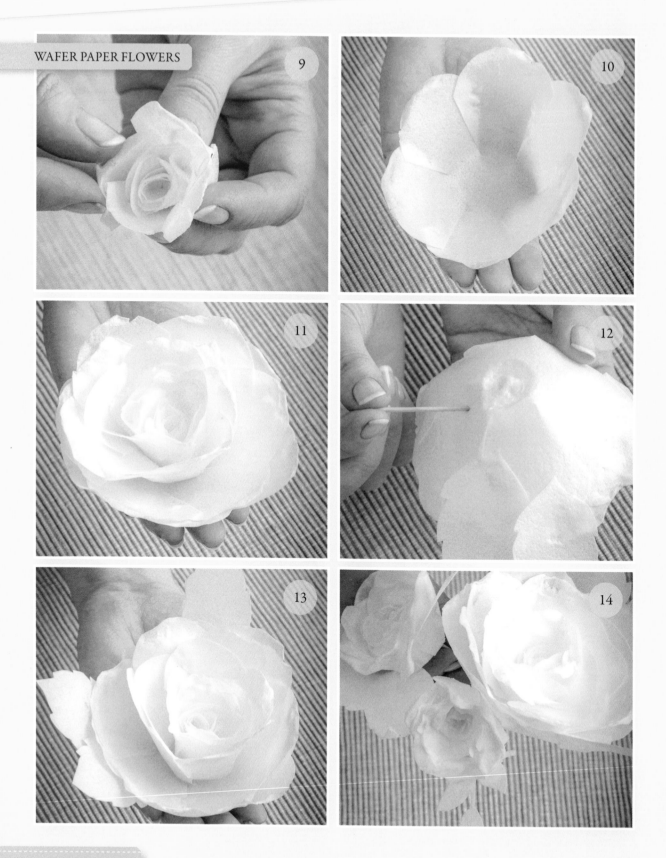

in the centre to form the heart of the rose. Set this aside for now.

6. Moisten the edges of the second of the size A cutouts, just as you did in step 2. Place the formed centre of the rose you made in steps 3 and 4 into the middle of this second cutout, letting it stick into place.

7. Repeat the curling and sticking procedure from steps 3 to 5 for this second cutout, bringing each petal up to the centre to create a further ring of petals. Set this aside again.

8. Dampen the edges of one of the size B cutouts, just as you did for the size A. Again, stick the formed centre into the middle of the new cutout.

   Repeat the petal curling and sticking procedure, thickening the rose to make a fuller bloom.

9. Repeat these processes with the other size B cutout and then both of the size C cutouts, adding each in turn. At this point the bloom will be 6 layers thick.

   Repeat the steps with the first of the size D cutouts. With these larger petals you can start to shape them slightly. You can do this either before or after they have been stuck to the bloom. To shape them, place your finger and thumb on the edge of the petal and pinch slightly so that it curls. This should create the shape of a rose petal.

10. Moisten the next size D cutout, but you'll be doing something slightly different with this one, so don't attach the rest of the rose to the centre just yet. Instead, pull each petal gently behind its neighbour, overlapping them by around 1 cm (⅜ inch), and stick them in place there to create a soft bowl shape. Form the petals as described above. If you find that the petals have dried out a little and feel too brittle to shape then just moisten them a little again.

11. Now stick the previously formed rose centre into the middle of the 'bowl'. Repeat the two steps above with the remaining size D and size E cutouts.

Note *If at any time you need to put the rose down while it is still damp, then make sure it will not stick to anything. Also take care to keep the unused wafer paper cutouts out of reach of any water spots, otherwise they will melt and stick together.*

----

12. While the rose is still damp, insert a cocktail stick into the centre through the bottom, make sure that it doesn't poke out of the top and become visible.

13. Cut out three or four large leaves and stick them to the back of the rose, making sure that they are visible from the front.

14. Set aside in a safe place to dry. This should only take 30 minutes or so. To make the smaller roses repeat the steps above but leave off some of the bigger layers.

    The smallest rose requires 2 each of templates A, B and C; while the medium rose requires 2 each of templates A, B and C plus a single D. Add the cocktail sticks to these in the same way as step 12. Cut out the leaves and stick these to the flowers.

SETTING UP

You can add the flowers to the cake before you set up; however, I would recommend placing the cake in position first before adding the flowers to prevent any damage in transit. Just insert the cocktail sticks into the cake where you wish to place the flowers until the bottom of the flower touches the surface of the cake.

Hello Cupcake!

DARK & WHITE CHOCOLATE CUPCAKES

While I admit that a large tiered cake can be showstopping, making cupcakes allows you the opportunity to present each guest with a little individual package of deliciousness. And these cupcakes are truly scrumptious.

If you feel daunted at the thought of making the sugar roses, don't worry! They are easy to make, if a little time consuming; however, if you really, really cannot face it you will find ready-made sugar roses in sugarcraft stores, online and now even in some supermarkets.

'HELLO CUPCAKE!' AT A GLANCE

BAKING SKILL: EASY

DECORATING SKILL: MEDIUM

Creating sugar-paste flowers can require a little practice. However if you use ready-made flowers, then it would be an easy-as-pie (or should that be cake?) project.

HOW FAR IN ADVANCE CAN IT BE MADE?

After creating this recipe I decided to sacrifice my waistline for Team Wedding and test the cakes every day for up to a week after baking, to see how long they would keep. It's a difficult job, but I wanted to be sure that if you were making this project that you wouldn't be left with stale cakes for your celebration. So here are my results: the dark chocolate in the cupcakes will keep them moist for up to four days after they have been baked; however, I think they are at their best up to three days (72 hours) after baking. The white chocolate cupcakes have a shorter shelf life and, while they are perfectly acceptable three days after baking, they are at their best up to or before the 48 hour mark. The cakes can be baked up to three months before the date needed and frozen, just make sure that they do not get squashed together in the freezer, as the cases will be ruined.

The cakes can be decorated as soon as they are cooled. The ganache and buttercream can be made up to a week in advance and stored in a refrigerator.

SETTING UP:

This shouldn't take any more than half an hour to set out, if the cakes are decorated in advance.

These cakes will last all day once set up, at normal room temperature. Do be aware though that if you are in a very hot venue (or if the cakes are in a window) the chocolate may start to melt (it would have to be uncomfortably hot). If the cakes are displayed in very humid conditions you may find that some of the sugar flowers start to wilt; however, as they are quite small decorations it shouldn't be too noticeable.

PORTIONS:

36 dark chocolate cakes,
36 white chocolate & Irish cream cakes.

PRICE PER PORTION: HIGH

TOTAL MAKING TIME:

13½ hours plus 2 hours cooling and 12 hours resting.

TOTAL BAKING TIME:

50 minutes.

DARK CHOCOLATE CUPCAKES

PREP: 45 minutes; BAKING: 20–30 minutes

500 ml (17 fl oz/2 cups) water
400 g (14 oz) good-quality dark chocolate (74% cocoa)
250 g (9 oz) unsalted butter
6 eggs
450 g (1 lb) raw (unrefined) sugar
3 teaspoons natural vanilla extract
2 teaspoons coffee extract
450 g (1 lb) self-raising flour

1. Place the water, chocolate and butter in a medium saucepan. Heat very gently until the chocolate and butter have melted, stirring constantly to make sure the chocolate doesn't settle at the bottom of the pan and burn. Once everything is melted take the pan off the heat and leave the mixture to cool.

2. Preheat the oven to 190°C (375°F). Line three 12-hole cupcake tins with cupcake cases.

3. Separate the eggs, putting the egg yolks into a large bowl with the sugar, and the egg whites in another grease-free bowl. Beat the egg yolks and sugar together until they are pale and fluffy.

4. Beat in the cooled chocolate mixture. Add in the vanilla and coffee extracts and mix well. Sift the flour and fold it into the mixture.

5. With clean beaters, whisk the egg whites until they have formed stiff peaks. Fold them into the cake batter, one-third at a time.

6. Fill the cupcake cases with the batter, so that they are around three-quarters full. The batter is quite runny so you may find this easier to do if you put the batter into a jug. Have a spoon at hand to catch any drips from the lip of the jug to prevent spots of batter falling onto the sides of the cases and creating burn marks once they are cooked.

7. Put all the cupcake tins into the oven at the same time and bake for 20 minutes, until a skewer inserted into the centre of a cupcake comes out clean. You may find the cakes at the top of the oven bake more speedily and the bottom tin may need a little longer. And if your oven has hot spots then the trays may need turning two-thirds of the way through cooking.

8. Cool the cakes in the tins for 5 minutes and then transfer them to a wire rack to cool completely.

GANACHE
PREP: 5 minutes plus 2 hours cooling time
COVERING: 20 minutes

500 g (1 lb 2 oz) good-quality dark chocolate (54% cocoa)
400 ml (14 fl oz) thick (double) cream

1. Make the ganache using the method described on page 34.

2. Leave the ganache to cool until it thickens, but is still pourable.

3. Pour the ganache over the cupcakes, making sure not to use so much that it starts to dribble over the edges of the cupcake cases.

4. Leave the cupcakes until the ganache has set, then store them in airtight containers until you need to decorate them.

WHITE CHOCOLATE AND IRISH CREAM CUPCAKES

PREP: 30 minutes; BAKING: 20 minutes

---

500 ml (17 fl oz/2 cups) water
400 g (14 oz) good-quality white chocolate
200 g (7 oz) butter
450 g (1 lb) self-raising flour
450 g (1 lb) light brown sugar
6 eggs
3 teaspoons natural vanilla extract
3 tablespoons Irish cream liqueur

1. Put the water, chocolate and butter in a medium saucepan. Heat very gently until the chocolate and butter have melted, stirring constantly to make sure the chocolate doesn't settle at the bottom of the pan and burn. Once everything is melted take the pan off the heat and leave the mixture to cool.

2. Preheat the oven to 190°C (375°F). Line three 12-hole cupcake tins with cupcake cases.

3. Separate the eggs, putting the egg yolks into a large bowl with the sugar, and the egg whites in another grease-free bowl. Beat the egg yolks and sugar together until they are pale and fluffy.

4. Beat in the cooled chocolate mixture, then add the vanilla extract and Irish cream and mix well. Sift the flour and fold it into the mixture.

5. With clean beaters, whisk the egg whites until they have formed stiff peaks. Fold them into the cake batter, one-third at a time.

6. Fill the cupcake cases with the batter to around three-quarters full. The batter is quite runny so you may find this easier if you put the batter in a jug. Have a spoon at hand to catch any drips from the lip of the jug to prevent spots of batter falling onto the sides of the cases and creating burn marks once they are cooked.

7. Put all the cupcake tins into the oven at the same time and bake for 20 minutes, until a skewer inserted in the centre of a cupcake comes out clean. The cakes at the top of the oven may bake more speedily and the bottom tin may need a little longer. If your oven has hot spots, turn the trays two-thirds of the way through cooking.

8. As soon as the cakes are out of the oven prick them all over the top and brush Irish cream over them. Cool the cakes in the tins for 5 minutes and then transfer them to a wire rack to cool completely.

WHITE CHOC BUTTERCREAM
PREP: 10 minutes; DECORATING: 30 minutes

225 g (8 oz) good-quality white chocolate
650 g (1 lb 7 oz) butter
650 g (1 lb 7 oz) icing (confectioners') sugar
5 tablespoons Irish cream liqueur

1. Melt the chocolate either in a microwave or in a heatproof bowl set over a saucepan of boiling water, then set aside to cool slightly.

2. Use an electric beater to beat the butter for around a minute, then add the icing sugar and beat for 3–5 minutes until it is paler and noticeably fluffier.

3. Beat in the cooled melted chocolate.

4. Beat in the Irish cream. If you find that the buttercream starts to curdle (or separate) then $\gg$

add more icing sugar and keep beating until the mixture comes together.

5. Put a heaped spoonful of the buttercream onto each cupcake. Then use a small palette knife to spread the buttercream over the cake. If you divide out the buttercream onto the cakes first with a

spoon and then spread them this will ensure that each cake is evenly frosted and that you won't run out of the buttercream for the last few cakes.

6. Once frosted, store the cakes in an airtight container until needed.

DECORATING THE CAKES

PREP: making modelling paste, 10 minutes plus 12 hours resting; making flowers, 10 hours; royal icing, 10 minutes; placing flowers, 1 hour

----

EQUIPMENT
rolling pin
cornflour (cornstarch)
2.5 cm (1 inch) and 1.7 cm (¾ inch) wide leaf cutters (preferably with veiners)
paintbrush or cocktail stick (toothpick)
800 g (1 lb 12 oz) modelling paste: use ready-made or see below for recipe
dusky pink and soft green food colouring

MODELLING PASTE
800 g (1 lb 12 oz) fondant icing
3½ teaspoons gum tragacanth

ROYAL ICING
PREP: 10 minutes
100 g (3½ oz) icing (confectioners') sugar
3 g (⅛ oz) meri-white powder
10–15 ml (⅜–½ fl oz) water

1. Make the modelling paste using the method described on page 34.

2. You will need 50 ml (1¾ oz) of edible glue (see page 54) or royal icing (see page 34).

3. If you have a PVC tablecloth then this is ideal to work on. If you don't have one, and find that the petals are sticking to the work surface or your fingers, then place a sheet of plastic wrap underneath and above the petals as you are forming the shapes.

4. Roll 6 hazelnut-size balls of modelling paste. Press down on one side of the ball with the pad of your thumb or finger (be careful not to mark the petal with your fingernail) to thin this out. You need to thin out around three quarters of the ball and the edge of the petal that you are pressing on should be as thin as you can make it.

5. Repeat the thinning process with the other 5 balls.

6. Pick up one petal and hold it with the thin edge pointing upwards. With your thumb, curl one side of the petal in on itself, and then keep curling to create the centre of the rose.

7. Take a second petal, again with the thin edge upwards. Wrap it around the first petal, with the midpoint of this new petal aligned with the lowest point in the　>>

centre piece. Pinch the top of the second petal between your thumb and forefinger and turn the edge of it outward slightly.

8. Add the third petal on the opposite side of the centre to the second. Shape the petal edge in the same manner. Note that, from this point on, each petal that you add should sit a little higher than the petals it surrounds, so that you can curl each successive petal outward slightly more, so that the rose bloom grows outward rather than upward.

9. Add the fourth petal with the centre at the join between the previous two petals. Add the fifth petal so that it slightly overlaps the back of the fourth. Repeat this process with the final petal, so that the sixth overlaps the fifth.

10. Carefully pinch off the excess fondant at the base of the bloom.

11. Leave the rose sitting upright to dry.

12. Create different sized roses by using fewer or adding more petals. You can choose the number of flowers to add to each cupcake, depending on how long you wish to spend making the roses. I would add one large flower to each cupcake or two smaller roses; however, you may wish to leave some cakes empty or add two or three flowers to each.

TO CREATE A COLOURED ROSE

1. Separate out 250 g (9 oz) of the modelling paste. Colour 50 g (1¾ oz) in a dark tone, 80 g (2¾ oz) in a medium tone and 120 g (4¼ oz) in a light tone of the colour you have chosen (I have used a dusky pink colour).

2. Make the rose in the same manner as above using the darkest tone in the centre of the rose, the medium tone for the middle petals and the lightest tone for the outer petals.

TO CREATE THE LEAVES

1. Divide 100 g (3½ oz) of the modelling paste into thirds and colour each third a different tone of soft green.

2. Roll the coloured paste out to 1 mm (⅟₃₂ inch) thick.

3. Cut out the leaves using the leaf cutter and press with the veiner. Set the leaves aside to dry either with the tip propped up slightly or after curling them over a small rolling pin (or an alternative item with a similar shape). Curl some face up and some face down. You will need at least two but preferably three leaves for each rose (the total number will depend on how many roses you wish to make). Make about half of the leaves of each shade of green in the small size and half in the large size.

If you are not using the flowers and leaves immediately, store them in a cardboard box.

DECORATE THE CUPCAKES

Add the roses and leaves to the cakes once they have been frosted, but before the icing firms up. Attach the leaves to the roses with a small dab of royal icing (use a paintbrush or cocktail stick) or a little edible glue.

TRANSPORTING

You can buy boxes for transporting cupcakes from specialty sugarcraft shops. Or you can use the tins you baked them in, as this will prevent any from toppling over.

SETTING UP

You can purchase or hire special tiered cake stands for displaying cupcakes, or you can display them on conventional cake stands. Alternatively, you can create a beautiful display on a table top.

MODELLING A FONDANT ROSE

4

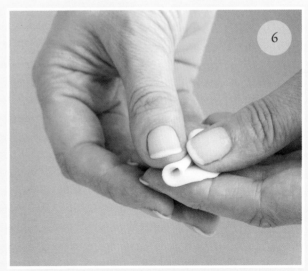

6

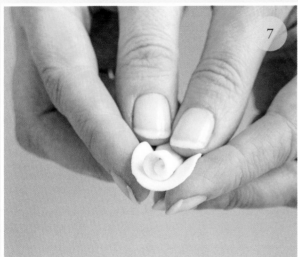

7

9

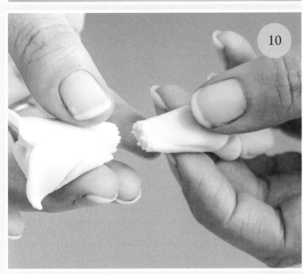

10

CREATING THE LEAVES

3

CHAPTER TWO

Putting on the glitz

Dynamite in diamonds, gorgeous in gold, or spangled in sequins: this is how you will find me attired every single day (when I'm not in jeans, T-shirt and a floury apron). I'm not ashamed to admit that I love glitter, and if I can add a splash of gold to a cake I am certain to go for it. Life is better with a bit of sparkle, and a wedding is the perfect time to unleash your inner diva. I'm thinking showbiz glam: red carpets, Champagne, truffles and a sprinkling of stardust from the silver screen. Who better to personify all that glamour than Elizabeth Taylor and Richard Burton: their romance was passionate, all-consuming and dripping with jewels. Happily, you don't need a Hollywood budget to add glitz and glamour to your wedding; sparkling edible sequins and fountains of gold can be achieved relatively cheaply and easily, so splash out a little. You're worth it...

THE CAKES

Going for Gold

CHOCOLATE & ORANGE CAKE

*This cake is golden in more ways than one.
I always associate oranges with sunny golden climes,
and in this cake the cheerful tanginess of oranges
marries perfectly with the richness of the chocolate,
all wrapped up in overflowing gold.*

I have to admit this is probably one of my favourite flavour
combinations; I'm sure it will please your guests equally well. Whatever
the weather on your big day, this cake is sure to bring out the sunshine.

'GOING FOR GOLD' AT A GLANCE

BAKING SKILL: EASY

DECORATING SKILL: MEDIUM

It can be a little tricky to create the sharp edges needed for this cake, but even if you can't get them perfect it will still look great.

HOW FAR IN ADVANCE CAN IT BE MADE?

You can bake the cake up to five days before the event and then cover and decorate it up to four days before the wedding. The cake layers can also be made up to three months in advance of the day and frozen. Leave them to defrost to room temperature before filling. The ganache can also be made up to a week in advance and stored in the refrigerator. You can warm it gently before you need it to soften it up. Just heat it in a microwave on the defrost setting until it is the desired consistency.

SETTING UP:

This shouldn't take more than 15 minutes to set out, as the cake is stacked and decorated beforehand so all you need to do is place it on a stand.

This cake can be set up the day before the event as long as the room temperature is normal (16–20°C or 60–68°F) and will not be subjected to any swings in temperature.

PORTIONS:

12 cm (5 inch) tier, 11 portions;
18 cm (7 inch) tier, 20 portions;
23 cm (9 inch) tier, 33 portions

PRICE PER PORTION: MEDIUM

TOTAL MAKING TIME:

This will vary depending on whether you bake each layer of each cake separately or three layers of one cake at a time. Up to 3¾ hours if baking individual layers or 1¼ hours if baking three layers at one time. You will need to bake three layers for each tier, a total of nine layers all together.

ON THE DAY:

Simply transport the assembled cake to the venue and place it on display.

CHOCOLATE & ORANGE CAKE

PREP: 30 minutes per cake.
Ingredients are for one layer: you require three layers for a tier.

12 CM (5 INCH) LAYERS: bake for 20–25 minutes
50 g (1¾ oz) unsalted butter
50 g (1¾ oz) unrefined sugar
zest and juice of half an orange
1 egg
50 g (1¾ oz) self-raising flour

18 CM (7 INCH) LAYERS: bake for 20–25 minutes
100 g (3½ oz) unsalted butter
100 g (3½ oz) unrefined sugar
zest and juice of half an orange
2 eggs
100 g (3½ oz) self-raising flour

23 CM (9 INCH) LAYERS: bake for 20–25 minutes
150 g (5½ oz) unsalted butter
150 g (5½ oz) unrefined sugar
zest and juice of 1 orange
3 eggs
150 g (5½ oz) self-raising flour

1. Preheat the oven to 190°C (375°F).

2. Grease and line the relevant-size cake tin(s).

3. Beat the butter and sugar together with the orange zest for at least 5 minutes. The mixture should become noticeably paler and take on a fluffy appearance.

4. Add the eggs (one at a time) and beat them in well. If the mixture stars to curdle, add a spoonful of the flour and beat again.

5. Sift the flour into the mixture and use a large spoon to gently fold it in.

6. Stir in the orange juice.

7. Spoon the batter into the cake tin. Bake for 20–25 minutes. The cake is ready when the top feels firm but springy to the touch and a cake tester or skewer inserted into the centre of the cake comes out clean.

8. Leave the cake to cool in the tin for 5 minutes, then turn out onto a wire rack to cool completely.

GANACHE

PREP: 5 minutes to make each batch (you can make them all together to save time),
plus up to 2 hours cooling time.

---

12 CM (5 INCH) TIER
350 g (12 oz) dark chocolate (54% cocoa)
175 ml (5½ fl oz/⅔ cup) orange juice

18 CM (7 INCH) TIER
500 g (1 lb 2 oz) dark chocolate (54% cocoa)
250 ml (9 fl oz/1 cup) orange juice

23 CM (9 INCH) TIER
950 g (2 lb 2oz) dark chocolate (54% cocoa)
475 ml (16 fl oz) orange juice

Make the ganache using the method described on page 34, substituting the orange juice for the cream. Allow to cool for 2 hours until the mixture is thick enough to spread but not solid.

Note *If you wish you can squeeze fresh orange juice to make the ganache; however, this will need a lot of oranges and be very time consuming. So I just used a good quality packet of juice, the kind with 'bits' in for added oranginess.*

LEVELLING AND FILLING THE LAYERS

PREP: 24 hours ahead, covering the drum, 10 minutes; 10–15 minutes per tier,
plus 20–30 minutes chilling per tier.

EQUIPMENT
28 cm (11 inch) covered cake drum (see page 41)
28 cm (11 inch), 23 cm (9 inch) and 18 cm (7 inch) cake boards
18 cm (7 inch) and 12 cm (5 inch) thin cake boards
cake leveller, or cocktail sticks (toothpicks) and a serrated knife
small palette knife (I would advise investing in one for this project as it will make it much easier, but you can still achieve a desirable effect with a substitute: see page 37)
cake scraper or alternative (see page 37)
marmalade: 12 cm tier, 1½ tablespoons; 18 cm tier, 2½ tablespoons; 23 cm tier, 3½ tablespoons

1. Process the marmalade in a food processor until the peel has been broken down and the marmalade has the consistency of a purée.

2. Level and fill the cakes using the method described on pages 37 and 42, with one layer of marmalade and one layer of ganache. Crumb-coat each layer and stand in the fridge for 15–20 minutes to harden.

3. Spread a thick layer of ganache over each tier using the method described on page 45.

DECORATING THE CAKES

PREP: 5–10 minutes per tier

EQUIPMENT
medium round-tipped paintbrush
⅓–¾ of a 25 ml (1 fl oz) bottle of edible gold paint
* for each tier*

1. Pour the gold paint onto the top of the cake tier. The layer of paint should be fairly thin, but thick enough so that you cannot see the ganache underneath. Spread it out with the paintbrush continuing up to and then over the edges.

2. You should find that drips are starting to form. Use the brush to control the drips, encouraging some to drip more by pulling them down a little; if you feel a drip is dripping too far, scrape a little of it off. If there are gaps in the line of drips then pour a little more paint in the relevant spaces. Leave the paint to dry overnight.

APPLY THE GOLD PAINT 1

ASSEMBLING THE TIERS

PREP: 10–15 minutes

Dowel and assemble the tiers using the method described on page 50.

Sparkling Celebration

SALTED CARAMEL CAKE

Salted caramel is the ambrosia of the gods. You can't throw a stick at the internet these days without hitting some delicious baked goods featuring it.

(If you miss the salted caramel with your stick, then odds are you hit a pulled pork dish, but that's for a different book.)

I am totally serious: salted caramel is the best sugar-based food, ever. A cake flavoured with this gooey delight and decorated with sparkling sequins is bound to be a big hit with your guests.

'SPARKLING CELEBRATION' AT A GLANCE

BAKING SKILL: MEDIUM

The cake itself is relatively easy to make, although you do have to caramelise the sugar; however, if you are nervous about this step there are plenty of ready-made salted caramels that you can find in a supermarket or an online store.

DECORATING SKILL: EASY

HOW FAR IN ADVANCE CAN IT BE MADE?

You can bake the cake six days before the event and then cover and decorate it five days before the wedding. The cake layers can also be made up to three months in advance of the day and frozen. Leave them to defrost to room temperature before filling with the buttercream. The buttercream can also be made up to three months in advance and frozen in airtight containers. Leave to defrost for 12 hours in a fridge before use; you will probably have to beat it to restore the fluffiness. The caramel will keep for two weeks in a refrigerator.

SETTING UP:

This shouldn't take any more than 15 minutes to set out, as the cake is stacked and decorated beforehand so all you need to do is place it on a stand. It can be set up the day before the event, as long as the conditions are normal (16–20°C or 60–68°F) and not cold, boiling, humid or damp, as this can affect the sugarpaste and buttercream.

PORTIONS:

15 cm (6 inch) tier, 14 portions;
20 cm (8 inch) tier, 25 portions

PRICE PER PORTION: MEDIUM

TOTAL MAKING TIME:

6 hours plus 3½ hours cooling and drying time.

TOTAL BAKING TIME:

From 1–3 hours.

ON THE DAY:

Simply transport the assembled cake to the venue and place it on display.

RECIPES

PREP: 20 minutes per layer. Ingredients quantities are for one layer
(you will need three layers to create each tier of the cake).

---

15 CM (6 INCH) CAKE: bake for 25–30 minutes

80 g (2¾ oz) unsalted butter
80 g (2¾ oz) light brown sugar
35 g (1¼ oz) caramel
2 eggs
½ teaspoon natural vanilla extract
100 g (3½ oz) self-raising flour
⅛ teaspoon salt flakes
2 tablespoons cream

20 CM (8 INCH) CAKE: bake for 30 minutes

125 g (4½ oz) butter
125 g (4½ oz) light brown sugar
50 g (1¾ oz) caramel
3 eggs
1 teaspoon natural vanilla extract
150 g (5½ oz) self-raising flour
¼ teaspoon salt flakes
4 tablespoons cream

1. Preheat the oven to 190°C (375°F). Grease and line the cake tin(s).

2. Beat the sugar and butter together until paler and fluffier: this should take around 3–5 minutes.

3. Beat in the caramel.

4. Add the eggs one at a time. If the mixture curdles then add a tablespoon of flour and keep beating.

5. Add the natural vanilla extract.

6. Sift the flour into the bowl and fold in well, until it is all incorporated.

7. Fold in the cream.

8. Spoon the batter into the tin(s) and bake for 25–30 minutes. The cake is ready when the top is springy to the touch and a skewer inserted into the middle comes out clean.

9. Allow the cake to cool in the tin for 5 minutes and then turn out onto a wire rack to cool completely.

CARAMEL

PREP: 10 minutes

600 g (1 lb 5 oz) sugar
50 g (1¾ oz) butter
500 ml (17 fl oz/2 cups) thick (double) cream
1 teaspoon flaky salt

1. Make the caramel using the method described on page 34.

2. Pour the caramel into a heatproof bowl and set aside to cool for at least an hour. The caramel can be made up to 2 weeks in advance and kept in the refrigerator.

CARAMEL BUTTERCREAM

PREP: 10 minutes per batch however, if you are using a hand whisk you may need to make the buttercream in several batches, so it will take you a little longer.

15 CM (6 INCH):
300 g (10½ oz) unsalted butter
300 g (10½ oz) unrefined icing (confectioners') sugar
150 g (5½ oz) caramel

20 CM (8 INCH):
450 g (1 lb) unsalted butter
450 g (1 lb) unrefined icing (confectioners') sugar
200 g (7 oz) caramel

1. Beat together the butter and icing sugar together until the mixture has turned very much paler and the mixture is light and fluffy: this should take around 5 minutes.

2. Add the caramel gradually, while still beating.

3. If the mixture starts to curdle, add more icing sugar and keep beating.

LAYERING AND ASSEMBLING THE TIERS

PREP: 24 hours ahead, covering the drum, 10 minutes; 15–20 minutes per tier

EQUIPMENT
25 cm (10 inch) covered cake drum (see page 41)
25 cm (10 inch) and 20 cm (8 inch) cake boards (uncovered for crumb coating)
15 cm (6 inch) thin cake board
cake leveller or cocktail sticks (toothpicks) and a serrated knife
palette knife (or other knife to spread the buttercream)
cake scraper (or ruler)
spirit level (optional)
rolling pin
cake smoothers (optional)
sharp knife
dowels
fondant: 20 cm (8 inch) cake, 800 g (1 lb 12 oz); 15 cm (6 inch), 600 g (1 lb 5 oz)

1. Level each tier of the cake using the method described on page 38. Warm the remaining caramel and brush it over each layer instead of sugar syrup.

2. Fill and crumb coat each tier with the caramel buttercream, following the instructions on pages 42 and 45.

3. Cover the cake with white fondant following the instructions on page 49.

4. Dowel and assemble the cake following the instructions on page 50.

DECORATING THE CAKE

PREP: 15 minutes to paint the sheets, an hour drying time, 2 hours 15 minutes to punch out the holes, 1 hour to attach the sequins to the cake.

EQUIPMENT

7 sheets of wafer paper
large paintbrush
25 ml (1 fl oz) bottle of dark silver edible paint
scissors
hole punch
water
tweezers

1. Paint the wafer sheets with the silver paint. You only need to paint one side of each sheet. Allow the paint to dry: at first the sheets will seem very elastic and then they will start to shrink as they dry out.

2. It can be tricky to find the right time to start punching the holes: you don't want to wait too long or the wafer paper will start to crinkle up and become too brittle to press out the sequins. At normal room temperature it should take about an hour for the edges to become dry enough to cut out. You can trim off any areas that are hard enough to cut and punch the circles while waiting for the other areas to dry. If you wish, you can speed the process up by drying out one sheet at a time with a hairdryer.

3. To attach the sequins to the cake, paint a small area at a time with water. Take a small handful of the sequins and press them against the wet area. Use the tweezers to turn around any sequins that are back to front, so that the silver-paint side is uppermost (although you will find that you don't need to do this with every single back-to-front sequin).

4. You can cover the whole cake with the sequins if you wish, but you will need to make more sequins. I have chosen to scatter the sequins over the areas of the cake where there may be flaws in the fondant covering, mostly around the edges.

5. Store the cake at room temperature until you need to display it.

MAKING & APPLYING SEQUINS

1+2

3

Up on Cloud Nine

GOLDEN MERINGUES

There is something very romantic about meringues: each one is like a small white fluffy cloud, and these particular ones have not so much a silver lining as a golden covering.

This would be a perfect project to serve to your guests as a dessert, just adding a bowl of cream and fresh berries. If you have a baking disaster then just crush up the meringues, stir them into the cream with the fruit and voilà! Eton mess.

'UP ON CLOUD NINE' AT A GLANCE

BAKING SKILL: MEDIUM

There are some people who can whip up a batch of meringues at the drop of a hat... I am not one of those people. I tested many different recipes to find a foolproof way of making meringues, and this one is fairly foolproof (and I am one such fool); however, you do need to make sure that the egg whites reach the right consistency.

DECORATING SKILL: EASY

HOW FAR IN ADVANCE CAN IT BE MADE?

You can make these around five or six days before the event. Alternatively, they can be baked and then frozen for a month in advance of the event. You need to store the meringues in the freezer very carefully so that they don't get crushed. I would suggest an airtight container.

SETTING UP:

This shouldn't take any more than 15 minutes to set out.

The meringues will last all day; however, if you are serving them with berries and fresh cream these items will need to be kept refrigerated until just before the meringues are served.

PORTIONS:

Makes about 28 meringues (depending on size).

PRICE PER PORTION: LOW

TOTAL MAKING TIME:

45 minutes

TOTAL BAKING TIME:

2½ hours

MERINGUE RECIPE

PREP: 20–25 minutes
BAKING: 2½ hours

12 egg whites (use pasteurised eggs)
1¼ teaspoons cream of tartar
615 g (1 lb 5½ oz) sugar

1. Preheat the oven to 120°C (250°F). Line three large baking trays with baking paper.

2. Put the egg whites and cream of tartar into the bowl of an electric mixer fitted with the whisk attachment and beat well until the egg whites form a stiff peak: this should only take a minute or so.

3. Keep beating and gradually add the sugar, one tablespoon at a time, until it has all been added. Keep beating until the sugar has dissolved into the egg white. If you rub a little of the mixture between your thumb and fingers it should feel smooth; any grittiness is undissolved sugar, so keep beating.

4. To form the meringues, take a heaped tablespoon of the mixture and use another spoon to drop the meringue onto the baking tray.

5. Put the meringues in the oven and bake for 2½ hours. If the meringues start to turn golden brown take them out of the oven.

6. Allow the meringues to cool on the trays.

DECORATING THE MERINGUES

PREP: 20 minutes

EQUIPMENT

3 sheets edible gold
medium round-tipped paintbrush
soft paintbrush
water
tweezers

Note *The gold sheets are incredibly thin and lightweight, so any breeze at all can lift them and give them folds. If this happens the gold will stick to itself and the sheet will be ruined. So make sure that all windows and doors are shut and that there is no draft from fans or air conditioners while you work.*

1. Use the round-tipped paintbrush to wet a small patch on the meringue. Don't use too much water or the meringue will melt: it should be damp rather than wet.

2. Tear a small piece of the gold from the sheet and lay it over the damp patch.

3. Brush the gold piece down with the soft paintbrush When all the meringues are decorated they can be stored in airtight containers until required.

APPLYING EDIBLE GOLD LEAF

1

2

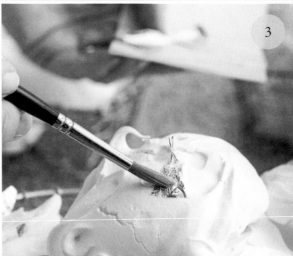

3

Chocolate Boom!

CHOCOLATE TIFFIN CAKE

*My heart always goes boom for chocolate,
and there can be nothing more boom-inducing
than a silky rich chocolate cake.*

This particular no-bake cake is perfect if you can't bear the thought
of slaving in a kitchen for hours, although it will take some time to
make the paper flower wreaths (you could use real flowers to save time).
Or you could hold a flower-making party: with seven friends you can
have it all done in an hour and have the evening left for fun!

'CHOCOLATE BOOM!' AT A GLANCE

BAKING SKILL: EASY

DECORATING SKILL: EASY

HOW FAR IN ADVANCE CAN IT BE MADE?

The large amount of chocolate in this cake will act as a preservative to the butter; however, I wouldn't make it more than seven days in advance because the chocolate isn't tempered, which means it can sometimes form a bloom (this isn't mould, just fat or sugar crystals forming on the cake) or the chocolate can shrink and crack. If it does bloom or crack, don't panic. Chocolate with a bloom is perfectly safe to eat, and you will be spraying the cake with gold so it will hide any defects. If the cake starts to crack, melt a small amount of chocolate and spread it over the offending fault (think of filling cracks in walls!) then, once the cake is sprayed, no-one will know!

SETTING UP:

This shouldn't take any more than half an hour to set out, if all the flowers are wired together in advance. You can set it up from the night before. There are no real issues with this particular cake at normal room temperature. Do be aware though that if you are in a very hot venue (or if the cake is in a very sunny window), the chocolate can melt.

PORTIONS:

12 cm (5 inch), 11 portions;
18 cm (7 inch), 20 portions;
23 cm (9 inch), 33 portions

PRICE PER PORTION: LOW

TOTAL MAKING TIME:

9 hours

ON THE DAY:

You do not need to worry about dowels, as the cakes are very firm and do not require any additional support. Just position the cake tiers on top of each other. Place the wreaths around the tiers and secure the ends of the wreath by wrapping the wires around each other.

CAKE RECIPE

*PREP: each cake will take 15–25 minutes to construct (it's not really baking)
and then at least two hours to set.*

12 CM (5 INCH)
275 g (9¾ oz) dark chocolate (54%), broken into small pieces
90 g (3¼ oz) unsalted butter, chopped into cubes
40 g (1½ oz) golden syrup (light treacle)
170 g (6 oz) biscuits (cookies). You can use any type of biscuit that takes your fancy: I prefer digestive biscuits (graham crackers or granita biscuits) but you could also use ginger biscuits, rich tea, amaretti or even puffed rice cereal.
75 g (2¾ oz) pistachio nuts
60 g (2 oz) mixed peel (mixed candied citrus peel)

18 CM (7 INCH)
450 g (1 lb) dark chocolate (54%), broken into small pieces
150 g (5½ oz) unsalted butter, chopped into cubes
75 g (2¾ oz) golden syrup (light treacle)
300 g (10½ oz) biscuits (see above)
125 g (4½ oz) chopped dried apricots
100 g (3½ oz) glacé cherries

23 CM (9 INCH)
900 g (2 lb) dark chocolate (54%), broken into small pieces
300 g (10½ oz) unsalted butter, chopped into cubes
150 g (5½ oz) golden syrup (light treacle)
650 g (1 lb 7 oz) biscuits (see above)
200 g (7 oz) chopped walnuts (or pecan nuts)
225 g (8 oz) raisins

1. Cut a 10 cm (4 inch) wide strip of baking paper long enough to cover the side and base of the cake tin and hang over the edge. Lay this in the base of the tin (with a portion of the strip hanging over the side at both ends) then line the tin as usual on top of this strip.

2. Melt the chocolate, butter and syrup together in a saucepan over low heat. Keep stirring to make sure that the chocolate doesn't burn on the bottom of the pan.

3. Break up the biscuits. The best way to do this is to put them in a food-grade bag (a large sandwich bag is perfect), secure the top of the bag so that the biscuit crumbs don't fly out all over your work surface, then bash the biscuits with a rolling pin (or the bottom of a pan). You should be left with mostly crumbs but there should also be some shards that are 2–3 cm (¾–1¼ inches) long. If the biscuit pieces are too big you may find the outside of the cake appears a little bit knobbly!

4. Add the biscuits, fruit and/or nuts to the chocolate mixture. Stir well until all the items are completely covered with chocolate.

5. Pour the mixture into the cake tin and press down.

6. Put the tin into a fridge until the mixture has hardened (at least 2 hours).

7. To release the cake, run a knife around the edge, then use the baking paper strip to lift the cake out. If you find it too difficult to release the cake then place the tin briefly in a bowl of hot water (make sure not to splash the top of the cake), as this will slightly melt the outside of the cake, making it easier to remove from the tin.

8. Remove the baking paper.

9. Cover the cake with plastic wrap and store in an airtight container until required. If you live in a very hot area then store the cake in the refrigerator.

DECORATING THE CAKE

PREP: making the flowers, 7½ hours; putting the flowers on the cake, 5 minutes

- -

EQUIPMENT
two 100 ml (3½ fl oz) cans of edible gold spray paint
white tissue paper
gold tissue paper
24-gauge florists' wire
1 cm (⅜ inch) wide white florists' tape
scissors
pencil
glue stick
template (see page 226)

Cover each tier of the cake with the gold spray. It is advisable to use a facemask and to spray outdoors if possible (although the paint is edible, you don't want to inhale it). You may find that you need two or three layers of the paint to create an even finish, but make sure you leave each layer to dry in between coats or you can create streaks.

TO MAKE THE FLOWERS:

1. Cut out a 5 cm (2 inch) square of white tissue paper and scrunch it into a tight ball.

2. Cut out a 5 cm (2 inch) square of gold tissue paper and wrap it over the scrunched-up ball of white tissue. Secure the ends by twisting wire around them.

3. Wrap a 5 cm (2 inch) length of florists' tape around the ends of the tissue paper and down part of the wire.

4. Press the rounded end of the tissue ball onto the work surface to flatten it slightly.

5. Cut a 35 cm x 4 cm (14 x 1½ inch) strip of white tissue paper. Concertina fold the paper at 3 cm (1¼ inch) intervals (the same width as the template).

6. Lay the template against the folded paper and draw a very light pencil line around the template. Cut out the petals, making sure not to cut all the way down the edges: there should be 1 cm (⅜ inch) of folded paper left intact at the bottom.

7. Unfold the petals and use the glue stick to apply glue along the bottom edge of the tissue paper.

8. Wrap the petals around the wire of the flower centre. Pleat the tissue paper slightly to create fuller flowers.

9. When all of the petals are around the flower, secure them in place with 20 cm (8 inches) of florists' tape, covering 10 cm (4 inches) of the wire as well. Snip off any excess wire.

10. Once you have made the required number of flowers, start to twist them together to make wreaths. Leave a 2–3 cm (¾–1¼ inch) gap between the base of the first flower and the petals of the next flower when you twist the covered wires together.

11. Do not complete the circle until the decoration is on the cake, in order to make sure that your wreath fits perfectly around the sides. You will need four wreaths of flowers: 30 cm (12 inches), 53 cm (21 inches), 67.5 cm (26½ inches) and 93 cm (36¾ inches).

12. You will need approximately 100 flowers to make the four wreaths, but you should make a few extra flowers in case you need to add some length to the wreaths when you are setting up.

Chapter Three

Laughing all the way to the altar

Love is serious business, but that doesn't mean that it has to take itself seriously. The reason I fell for my special person was his sense of humour, and he still makes me laugh every day. While I do admit that a wedding ceremony calls for a certain solemnity, especially when exchanging vows, there is plenty of scope during the rest of the day to indulge in humour. Think about the pairings to be found in 1940s screwball comedies: Jimmy Stewart and Margaret Sullavan or Katharine Hepburn and Cary Grant. These are couples who liked to banter and joke around with razor-sharp wit and affection. The projects in this chapter should appeal to a kooky couple, who don't take themselves seriously and enjoy laughing together.

The Cakes

Popping the Question

CHOCOLATE POPCORN CAKE

I like to imagine that if the Cat in the Hat were to be married or if Tom and Jerry were to tie the knot (we all know they love each other really) this would be the style of cake they would choose.

The great height of this cake gives it a cartoon quality that tickles my fancy, and the popcorn sends me back to my childhood watching cartoons in the cinema before the main feature. Although it may look precarious, with the right support this cake is a cinch to make.

'POPPING THE QUESTION' AT A GLANCE

BAKING SKILL: MEDIUM

This is a fairly simple chocolate cake with buttercream icing. Experience will come in handy when making the caramel.

DECORATING SKILL: EASY

The trickiest part is putting the cake together.

HOW FAR IN ADVANCE CAN IT BE MADE?

The cake can be baked up to three days before the wedding, or baked in advance up to three months beforehand and frozen. The buttercream can be made up to a week in advance and kept in a refrigerator.

SETTING UP:

A matter of minutes to transfer the cake from a box onto its stand. You can set it up from 24 hours before it is required, so you can set it up the night before (as long as it is in a room at a normal temperature and not subject to extreme temperature or temperature swings).

PORTIONS:

You will need two layers per tier and the cake is made up of three tiers, so six layers in total. Each 20 cm (8 inch) tier yields 25 portions (75 portions in total).

PRICE PER PORTION: LOW

TOTAL MAKING TIME:

4 hours

TOTAL BAKING TIME:

5½ hours (if baking one layer at a time).

ON THE DAY:

Simply transport the assembled cake to the venue and put it on display. The cake will be fine at room temperature until required, but it can be stored in a fridge or cool room if needed.

CHOCOLATE CAKE RECIPE

PREP: 20 minutes per layer;
BAKING TIME: 55 minutes per layer. Ingredients
quantities are for each layer (you will need six layers).

---

200 g (7 oz) dark chocolate (70%)
130 g (4½ oz) caster (superfine) sugar
130 g (4½ oz) butter
4 eggs
1 teaspoon natural vanilla extract
130 g (4½ oz) self-raising flour
¼ teaspoon salt

1. Preheat the oven to 170°C (325°F). Grease and line a 20 cm (8 inch) round cake tin(s).

2. Melt the chocolate in a heatproof bowl over a saucepan of simmering water and then set aside to cool slightly.

3. Beat the sugar and butter together until paler and fluffier: this should take 3–5 minutes.

4. Add the eggs one at a time. If the mixture curdles, add a tablespoon of flour.

5. Add the vanilla extract and the melted chocolate and beat in well.

6. Sift the flour and salt into the bowl and fold it in well, until it is all incorporated.

7. Spoon the batter into the prepared tin and bake for 50–55 minutes. The cake is ready when the top is springy to the touch and a skewer inserted into the middle comes out clean.

8. Leave the cake to cool in the tin for 5 minutes, then turn out onto a wire rack to cool completely.

POPCORN BUTTERCREAM

PREP: 20 minutes plus 30 minutes cooling time.
Ingredients are per tier (you need three batches
to create this cake).

CARAMEL POPCORN
100 g (3½ oz) caster (superfine) sugar
1 tablespoon thick (double) cream
525 g (1 lb 2½ oz) butter
30 g (1 oz) popped salted popcorn (if you pop your own do
  check that there are no unpopped kernels as you do not want
  any of your guests to break their teeth on your cake!)
500 g (1 lb 2 oz) icing (confectioners') sugar
1 teaspoon natural vanilla extract

1. Make the caramel using the caster sugar, cream and 25 g (1 oz) of the butter, following the method described on page 34.

2. Put the popcorn in a large heatproof bowl and pour the caramel over. Stir until all the popcorn is covered, then tip it out onto a baking tray lined with baking paper.

3. Allow to cool for about 30 minutes (or, to speed up the process, put the tray in a refrigerator).

4. When cooled, break up the caramel popcorn into smaller pieces, put them in a food processor or blender and blitz until they are the consistency of breadcrumbs.

5. Beat the remaining 500 g (1 lb 2 oz) of butter with the icing (confectioners') sugar until pale and fluffy.

6. Beat in the vanilla.

7. Beat in the caramel popcorn crumbs.

LEVELLING AND FILLING THE LAYERS

PREP: 24 hours ahead, covering the drum, 10 minutes; 10–15 minutes per tier.

EQUIPMENT
23 cm (9 inch) or 25 cm (10 inch) covered cake drum
three 25 cm (10 inch) cake boards (for crumb coating)
two 18 cm (7 inch) thin cake boards
cake leveller, or cocktail sticks (toothpicks) and a serrated knife
small palette knife (I would advise investing in one for this
  project as it will make it much easier, but you can still
  achieve a desirable effect with a substitute: see page 37)
cake dowels
edible-ink pen

1. Level the layers using the method described on page 37.

2. Using the same method (either with a cake leveller or cocktail sticks) cut each layer in half horizontally. Each tier will consist of four half-layers of cake with buttercream sandwiched between them. Try to make every layer the same height, as this will give your cake a more professional appearance.

3. Use a quarter of the buttercream for each layer of filling (the quantities above will fill one tier, so make three batches), remembering to set two of the tiers on to thin 18 cm (7 inch) cake boards before you start filling. Try to make each layer of filling equal. Carefully spread the buttercream on the tiers, leaving a 5 mm (¼ inch) gap around the edge. The weight of the next layer placed on top should spread the buttercream out to the edge.

ASSEMBLING THE TIERS

PREP: 10–15 minutes

Dowel and assemble the tiers using the method described on page 50.

DECORATING THE CAKE

PREP: 10 minutes plus an hour cooling time

INGREDIENTS
300 g (10½ oz) caster (superfine) sugar
6 tablespoons thick (double) cream
50 g (1¾ oz) butter
60 g (2¼ oz) popped salted popcorn

1. Cut out a 20 cm (8 inch) disc of baking paper. Make the caramel using the method described on page 34, using the sugar, butter and 3 tablespoons of the cream.

2. Put the popcorn in a heatproof bowl, pour half of the caramel over it and stir until every little bit of popcorn is covered with caramel. Allow to cool slightly.

3. When the popcorn is cool enough to touch (but hasn't yet become solid), tip it out onto the disc of baking paper. Form a mountain of the popcorn and leave it to cool completely and harden.

4. Remove the tower from the baking paper, then transfer 'Mount Popcorn' onto the top of the cake.

5. Reheat the remaining caramel until it comes to the boil. Remove from the heat and add the remaining cream. Stir well and allow to cool slightly. Pour it over the popcorn on the cake.

PLACING 'MOUNT POPCORN'

4

5

I Do!

CHOCOLATE BROWNIES & CARAMEL BLONDIES

There will be more than just two people saying 'I do' at your wedding if you make these delicious treats for your guests: they will be 'I do-ing' all over the place!

Everybody loves a chocolate brownie and if they don't, then they are bound to fall for a caramel blondie. It's sure to be love at first bite.

'I DO!' AT A GLANCE

BAKING SKILL: EASY

DECORATING SKILL: EASY

HOW FAR IN ADVANCE CAN IT BE MADE?

Made up to five days in advance, the brownies and blondies will still taste fresh if stored in an airtight container. I would advise you to keep them as a whole slab rather than cutting them up into squares, as this will keep them fresher longer. They can be baked and then frozen for up to three months. If you are going to freeze them, keep them as a whole slab. As soon as they have cooled, take off the baking paper and cover each slab in two layers of plastic wrap, then cover with a layer of foil. Be careful not to freeze too many slabs on top of each other as you may find the bottom one will get squished! Make sure that one portion has totally frozen before you put another one on top and you should find they keep their shape.

SETTING UP:

It will take about half an hour. Once the brownies and blondies have been cut into portions, do not leave them uncovered for any more than 4 hours, as you will find they will go stale. They will keep longer if you place them on plates or a cake stand and then cover them with plastic wrap, which can be removed just before displaying them for serving. Or you could find domed cake stands, which should keep the goodies fresh for up to 8 hours.

PORTIONS:

36 dessert-size portions or 64 party portions.

PRICE PER PORTION: MEDIUM

TOTAL MAKING TIME:

2 hours

TOTAL BAKING TIME:

1 hour 20 minutes

BROWNIES AND BLONDIES

Each recipe produces two tins worth of batter, so obviously if you only have one tin or are having a very small wedding then halve the quantities. The slabs can be cut into portions in whatever size you require. If you are serving your guests dessert, then cut each slab into 16 portions, if you want to dish up the goodies as the dessert then cut each slab into nine portions. These would be great served with a bowl of fruit and whipped cream, which should be stored in a refrigerator to keep them fresh and put out with the brownies and blondies at the very last minute.

BROWNIES

PREP: 20 minutes; BAKING: 30 minutes

400 g (14 oz) dark chocolate (70%), broken into small pieces
400 g (14 oz) unsalted butter, chopped into small cubes
6 eggs
350 g (12 oz) golden caster (superfine) sugar
3 teaspoons natural vanilla extract
½ teaspoon coffee flavouring (optional)
170 g (6 oz) plain (all-purpose) flour
75 g (2¾ oz) unsweetened cocoa powder
½ teaspoon salt flakes

1. Preheat the oven to 180°C (350°F).

2. Line two 23 cm (9 inch) square tins with baking paper.

3. Put the chocolate and butter into a saucepan over low heat and gently heat them together until they have melted. Stir constantly to prevent the chocolate from burning on the bottom: if you suspect that this is happening, reduce the heat. When melted, remove from the heat and leave the mixture to cool slightly in the pan.

4. Beat the eggs and sugar together in a large bowl, until the mixture has doubled in size and become lighter in colour and fluffy. If you are using a handheld beater or standing electric mixer this will take about 5 minutes on full power. If you are whisking by hand it may take much longer, depending on your muscle strength!

5. Incorporate the vanilla and coffee flavouring (if using) into the egg mixture.

6. Pour the melted chocolate mixture into the egg mixture, then use a rubber spatula to fold the two mixtures together. Keep folding until both the mixes are fully incorporated.

7. Mix together the flour and cocoa powder and sift them over the combined mixture; add the salt then fold in the flour mixture until it is fully incorporated.

8. Divide the mixture between the prepared tins: each tin should hold roughly 850 g (1 lb 14 oz) of batter.

9. Bake for 30 minutes. You can test to see if the brownies are ready by inserting a cake tester or skewer into the middle of the cake; however, this is not the same as testing a sponge cake. The skewer may have some moist crumbs attached to it (rather than being totally clean). Another way to test if the brownies are ready is to shake each tin gently, if the middle of the cake is still very wobbly put it back into the oven for 5 minutes. You will find that the brownies will keep cooking once they are out of the oven, so you must be very careful not to overcook them.

10. Allow to cool in the tin.

11. As soon as it is cool, take the slab out of the tin, cover in plastic wrap and store in an airtight container or cover with a layer of foil and freeze.

BLONDIES

PREP: 30 minutes plus 1 hour for cooling;
BAKING: 50 minutes

450 g (1 lb) unsalted butter
4 eggs
300 g (10½ oz) light brown sugar
300 g (10½ oz) dark brown sugar
4 teaspoons natural vanilla extract
600 g (1 lb 5 oz) plain (all-purpose) flour
4 teaspoons baking powder
¼ teaspoon salt flakes

CARAMEL

200 g (7 oz) caster (superfine) sugar
200 g (7 oz) thick (double) cream
30 g (1 oz) unsalted butter, cut into small chunks
1 teaspoon salt flakes

1. Make the caramel using the method described on page 34. Leave the caramel to cool for at least 1 hour: the caramel can be made up to 2 weeks in advance and kept in the refrigerator.

2. Preheat the oven to 180°C (350°F).

3. Line two 23 cm (9 inch) square cake tins with baking paper.

4. Melt the butter and then set aside to cool slightly.

5. Beat the eggs with the combined sugars. Break up any big lumps in the sugar before you start whisking. The volume should double in size and become very pale and fluffy: it will take 3–5 minutes if you are using an electric handheld or standing mixer, but it may take much longer if you are doing this with a hand whisk!

6. Fold in the cool melted butter and the vanilla until they are totally incorporated into the egg mixture.

7. Mix the flour and baking powder together in a bowl and then sift them over the batter.

8. Fold the flour into the batter until it is totally incorporated and you can't see any of the flour.

9. Divide half of the mixture (about 900 g or 2 lb) between the tins and smooth it down so it has a flat surface.

10. Pour the caramel sauce into the pans over the layer of blondie batter (about 200 g or 7 oz in each tin). Then gently tip the tin in all directions to create an even layer of the caramel.

11. Divide the remaining batter between the tins on top of the caramel. You will find this easier if you spoon it on in lumps and then gently spread it over the tin.

12. Try to cover up all of the sauce with the batter, otherwise it can bubble up during baking and burn slightly.

13. Bake for 45–50 minutes. As with the brownies, it can be difficult to tell if the blondies are cooked. A skewer inserted into the centre of the cake is likely to come out covered in the sauce and so give you the impression that the blondie is not cooked. The easiest way to tell is to give the tin a little shake: the centre should have a very slight wobble but not too much. Also if you gently press the surface of the blondie it should have a slight give without feeling as if there is liquid under the surface. Do bear in mind that the blondie will continue cooking as it cools in the tin.

14. Leave to cool in the tin.

15. As soon as it is cool, remove the slab from the tin and cover it in plastic wrap. Store in an airtight container or add a layer of foil and freeze.

TO SERVE

Using a large sharp knife, slice off the outside edges of the blondies and brownies. Measure the width of the slabs and divide by four for a party portion size or three for a dessert portion size. Cut the slabs into the relevant portions. Clean the knife frequently while slicing to ensure a smooth cut. Stack the squares in pyramids on cake plates or stands: you can mix the flavours together or keep them separate. If you put the baked goodies on the plates the night before and cover them with plastic wrap they will stay fresh.

TO DECORATE

Use a mix of delicate garden flowers and cut flowers to decorate the platters. Put the central flowers in a jam jar, and add more flowers in small jam jars and tea light holders. This will prolong the life of the flowers and if you set up the display in the morning it will still be fresh and beautiful when you come to serving. Cut stems at a sharp angle to stop wilting. Cover the whole display in loose plastic wrap to keep the baked goods fresh. If you're using crystallised or paper flowers, they can be set up in the morning.

Key Largo

COCONUT & LIME CAKE

Another great 1940s pairing was Humphrey Bogart and Lauren Bacall who enjoyed razor-sharp repartee together on and off the screen.

I can envision Bogie and Baby sailing away to Key Largo, each with a cocktail in hand, wearing deck shoes and jaunty hats and looking ever so chic. This recipe will create the perfect cake for a tropical wedding. And if you are tying the knot somewhere less than tropical (anywhere in the UK, during the summer) then it's sure to give your guests a totally tropical taste sensation.

'KEY LARGO' AT A GLANCE

BAKING SKILL: EASY

DECORATING SKILL: EASY

HOW FAR IN ADVANCE CAN IT BE MADE?
The cake layers can be made up to five days before the wedding, and filled and decorated up to four days before the wedding. The cake layers can also be made up to three months in advance of the day and frozen. Leave them to defrost at room temperature before filling with the buttercream. The decorations can be made up to two weeks in advance depending on the humidity in your area. Store them in an airtight container with a sachet of silica gel if necessary.

SETTING UP:
Takes a matter of minutes, all you need to do is place it on display at your venue.
You can set up the night before or on the morning of the wedding as long as the cake is not subjected to swings of temperature or humidity.

PORTIONS:
15 cm (6 inch), 12 portions;
20 cm (8 inch), 28 portions;
25 cm (10 inch) 46 portions.

PRICE PER PORTION: LOW

TOTAL MAKING TIME:
5½ hours

TOTAL BAKING TIME:
5½ hours

ON THE DAY:
Transport to the venue and place on a display stand or table.

RECIPES

PREP: 20 minutes per layer. Ingredient quantities are for one layer: you require three layers for each tier.

- -

15 CM (6 INCH) CAKE LAYER: bake for 30 minutes

50 g (1¾ oz) unsalted butter
zest of 1 lime
25 g (1 oz) creamed coconut (or the solids from coconut cream)
50 g (1¾ oz) light brown sugar
1 egg
60 g (2¼ oz) self-raising flour
2 tablespoons coconut milk

20 CM (8 INCH) CAKE LAYER: bake for 30–35 minutes

100 g (3½ oz) unsalted butter
zest of 1 lime
50 g (1¾ oz) creamed coconut (or the solids from coconut cream)
100 g (3½ oz) light brown sugar
2 eggs
115 g (4 oz) self-raising flour
4 tablespoons coconut milk

25 CM (10 INCH) CAKE LAYER: bake for 35–40 minutes

200 g (7 oz) unsalted butter
zest of 2 limes
100 g (3½ oz) creamed coconut (or the solids from coconut cream)
200 g (7 oz) light brown sugar
4 eggs
230 g (8 oz) self-raising flour
8 tablespoons coconut milk

1. Preheat the oven to 190°C (375°F).

2. Grease and line the cake tin(s) with baking paper.

3. Beat the butter, lime zest, creamed coconut and sugar together until they are creamed, this will take about 3 or 4 minutes. If the creamed coconut is too hard then you can soften it slightly by warming it in the microwave for a few seconds; make sure that you don't overheat it as you don't want it too liquid.

4. Add the eggs one by one (if the mixture curdles, add a teaspoon of flour).

5. Sift the flour into the bowl and fold into the mixture with a spoon or spatula.

6. Fold in the coconut milk.

7. Spoon the mixture into the prepared tin and bake for 30–40 minutes (the smaller cake will take less time and the larger cake will need to be in for at least 35 minutes), until a skewer inserted into the centre of the cake comes out clean.

8. Allow the cake to cool in the tin for 10 minutes, then turn out onto a wire rack, remove the baking paper and allow to cool completely.

- -

SUGAR SYRUP

PREP: 10 minutes
125 ml (4 fl oz/½ cup) water
125 g (4½ oz) caster (superfine) sugar
zest of 2 limes

Use the method described on page 34 to make sugar syrup, adding the lime zest when you remove the pan from the heat.

LIME BUTTERCREAM

PREP: 10 minutes per batch (if you are mixing the buttercream with a hand whisk rather than a standing electric mixer you will find it easier to make the larger amounts in batches.)

15 CM (6 INCH) CAKE

250 g (9 oz) unsalted butter
250 g (9 oz) icing (confectioners') sugar
zest and juice of 2 limes
green food colouring (optional)

20 CM (8 INCH) CAKE

450 g (1 lb) unsalted butter
450 g (1 lb) icing (confectioners') sugar
zest and juice of 3 limes
green food colouring (optional)

25 CM (10 INCH) CAKE

700 g (1 lb 9 oz) unsalted butter
700 g (1 lb 9 oz) icing (confectioners') sugar
zest and juice of 4 limes
green food colouring (optional)

1. Beat together the butter, icing sugar and lime zest until the mixture has turned very much paler and the mixture is light and fluffy: this should take around 5 minutes.

2. Add the lime juice gradually, while still beating.

3. Add the food colouring if you wish, adding a small amount at a time until you reach the desired tone. Make sure that all your batches of buttercream are the same colour to avoid a stripy effect when the cake is cut.

LEVELLING AND FILLING THE LAYERS

PREP: 15–20 minutes per tier

- -

EQUIPMENT

30 cm (12 inch), 25 cm (10 inch) and 20 cm (8 inch) cake boards, for crumb-coating
20 cm (8 inch) and 15 cm (6 inch) thin cake boards
cake leveller or a large serrated knife and cocktail sticks (toothpicks)
palette knife (or other knife to spread the buttercream)
cake scraper (or ruler)
spirit level (optional)

Fill and crumb-coat the tiers using the method described on pages 42 and 45.

COVERING THE CAKES

PREP: 24 hours ahead, covering the drum, 10 minutes; 15–20 minutes per tier

- -

EQUIPMENT

30 cm (12 inch) covered cake drum (see page 41)
rolling pin
spacers (optional, see page 38)
sharp knife
smoothers (optional)
cornflour (cornstarch)
white fondant: 15 cm (6 inch), 600 g (1 lb 5 oz); 20 cm (8 inch), 800 g (1 lb 12 oz); 25 cm (10 inch), 1.25 kg (2 lb 12 oz)

Cover the cakes with fondant using the method described on page 49.

DECORATING THE CAKE

PREP: 1 hour

EQUIPMENT

four A4 (Letter) sheets of wafer paper
scissors
pot of water
ruler
non-toxic pencil
edible-ink pens: navy blue, sky blue and yellow

1. Dowel and assembled the tiers, following the instructions on page 50.

2. For the bottom tier, cut two strips of wafer paper measuring 9 x 30 cm (3½ x 12 inches) and one strip 9 x 23 cm (3½ x 9 inches). Join them together to make one long strip. To stick the strips together, moisten one edge very slightly (if you wet it too much it will dissolve). Overlap the edges by 5 mm (¼ inch) or less.

3. Measure 3 cm (1¼ inches) from the long edge of the strip and make a small mark with the pencil. Then measure 6 cm (2½ inches) from the edge and make a mark here too. Place scrap paper along the line where you have made the 3 cm mark: this will provide an edge for you to work up to without drawing a pencil line, as you would not be able to erase this off the wafer paper. You can draw any pattern that you like, using the navy blue pen: I have drawn polka dots on the first third. (Note: Some wafer papers have a textured side and a smooth side; draw on the smooth side.)

4. Move the strip of paper up to the 6 cm mark and draw the next pattern: here I have drawn four rows of small vertical dashes. Remove the paper and draw the pattern in the final third. I have drawn starbursts and dots.

5. To make the collar for the middle tier, cut one strip of wafer paper measuring 9 x 30 cm (3½ x 12 inches) and

two strips of wafer paper measuring 9 x 19 cm (3½ x 7½ inches). Join the strips together to make one long strip using the same technique described in step 2.

6. Use the sky blue pen to make the pattern using the same technique as steps 3 and 4.

7. Cut two strips to create the decoration for the top tier, one measuring 9 x 30 cm (3½ x 12 inches) and one strip 9 x 20 cm (3½ x 8 inches). Stick one end of each strip to the other strip using the same process as in step 2.

8. Create the pattern with the yellow pen using the same technique as steps 3 and 4.

9. Attach the patterned strips around each tier of the cake by moistening one end of the strip and sticking the other end to it.

MAKE THE PATTERN 6

Fiesta Matrimonio

PIÑATA

I think of a piñata like the Statue of Liberty: serene and beautiful on top, but there is a lot going on underneath to hold it all together.

Piñatas are enjoying an upswing (pun intended) in their popularity, and not just with children. I have witnessed, first-hand, hordes of adults arguing over who gets the next swing, and seen the glory heaped on the one who breaks it. This is the perfect 'recipe' for someone who really doesn't want to bake a wedding cake and is looking for a fun alternative. It's really easy to make.

'FIESTA MATRIMONIO' AT A GLANCE

BAKING SKILL: NON-EXISTENT!

CRAFTING SKILLS: EASY

The 'filling' in the cake is up to you: add sweets or wrapped chocolates and lots of glitter and confetti, but make sure they can stand up to a good whacking; the finest Belgian truffles might make for an exquisite treat, but they'll look much less appealing after a good few whacks from a burly groomsman. You can add the sweets when you are constructing the piñata, but if you want to make it well in advance, leave the flap open, add the sweets when you need to, then glue the flap shut. Of course you can make a smaller piñata if you wish, just use the same proportions but reduce the size by 30 per cent. You will also need an implement to hit the piñata with. Anything long and thin will serve the task; a baseball bat, an old sawn-down broom handle or just a length of thick dowel from your local DIY shop. But do make sure that you keep the crowds back while the hitter is in full swing: you don't want to end your big day with a trip in an ambulance!

HOW FAR IN ADVANCE CAN IT BE MADE?
As early as you wish.

PORTIONS:
As many as you require.

PRICE PER PORTION: LOW
The price of making the piñata is low, especially if you recycle a cardboard box; however, the overall cost will depend on the price of the sweets you put inside.

TOTAL MAKING TIME:
7½ hours

CONSTRUCTING THE PIÑATA

MAKING TIME: 2½ hours

EQUIPMENT

cardboard: you need to use a strong corrugated cardboard such as a cardboard box; you can buy sheets of this or reuse old cardboard boxes, in which case you will need three or four large boxes.

hot-glue gun: you will need about 11 packs of glue sticks

scissors

ruler

parcel (packing) tape (optional)

6 packs of white crepe paper, 250 x 50 cm (98½ x 20 inches) each

wrapped sweets or chocolates

glitter and confetti (optional)

3 m (118½ inches) white ribbon, for hanging

START WITH THE BOTTOM TIER

1. Cut out two 52 cm (20¾ inch) diameter circles from corrugated cardboard. You can use an object to draw around (I used a very large cake board) or go old-school and tie a pencil to a piece of string, pin the other end of the string down on the cardboard so that the string measures half the diameter—26 cm (10½ inches)—and draw each circle by sweeping it around the centre at full stretch. If using cardboard boxes for the material, don't be too concerned if you have to cut across a crease in the card to get something of the right size, as the sides of the 'cake' will reinforce any weakness.

2. Cut a strip of cardboard measuring 37 x 170 cm (14½ x 67 inches). Mark a line 6 cm (2½ inches) from one long edge along the whole length (this is the top edge). Make a series of cuts from the top edge down to the line you have marked, approximately 2 cm (¾ inch) apart, so that you create a thick fringe all along the top edge. Turn the strip over and repeat this process for the bottom edge.

3. Roll the strip up and then allow it to unroll again: this will help to form the strip around the circle base. Fold the fringes inward.

4. Line up the folded edge with the circumference of the base circle, then glue the folded fringe down. Glue along the edge of the circle

5. Once you have glued all the way around the circle you should be left with an overlapping flap, so cut off the fringing on this section.

6. Make sure that there is a big enough gap at the flap to insert the sweets.

7. Glue the second circle to the top of the strip. If there are any areas that don't stick too well then tape up the gaps with the packing tape, but don't make it so solid that it won't ultimately split when hit – that is the point, after all.

MIDDLE TIER

8. For this tier you'll only need to cut out a single 42 cm (16½ inch) circle and a strip 37 x 134 cm (14½ x 52¾ inches). If you want to create a flap on this tier make the strip 7 cm (2¾ inches) longer. Cut and fold the fringe and roll the strip in the same manner as described above.

9. Place the 42 cm circle in the centre top of the first 'tier' of the cake and trace around it.

10. Glue the fringes of the strip around the drawn circle to form the wall of the second tier.

11. Glue the 42 cm circle to the top of the strip, again using packing tape if you need to reinforce any edges. (Leave a flap if you require one.)

TOP TIER

12. Cut out a single 32 cm (12⅝ inch) diameter circle and a 37 x 100 cm (14½ x 39½ inch) strip. If you want to create a flap on this tier, make the strip 5 cm (2 inches) longer. Cut and fold the fringing and roll the strip in the same manner as described above. Repeat steps 9 and 10 as for the middle tier. Don't stick the top on yet!

13. Cut the ribbon in half to create two 150 cm (50 inch) lengths. Make a hole 4 cm (1½ inches) down from the top edge on one side of the top tier, and then another hole exactly opposite it.

14. Push the end of one length of ribbon through one hole, tie a triple knot in the end of the ribbon that is on the inside of the tier and then add a blob of glue to keep it securely in place.

15. Push the other piece of ribbon through the other hole (from the outside) and repeat, so that when they are tied together the ribbons will form a loop for hanging, but do not do this until you have decorated the piñata.

16. Glue the top of the tier in place. Now you are ready to start decorating the outside.

CONSTRUCTING THE PIÑATA

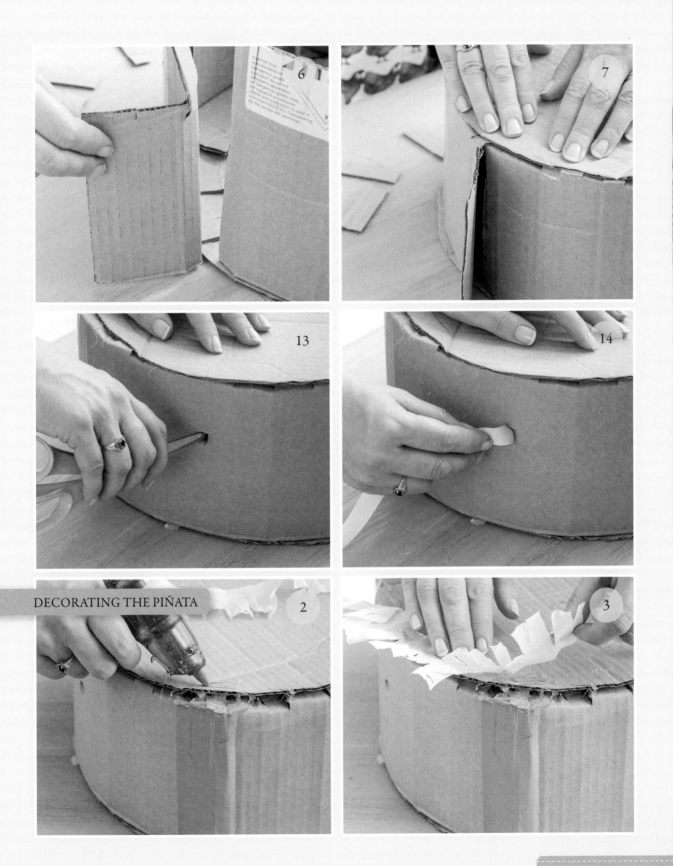

DECORATING THE PIÑATA

DECORATING THE PIÑATA

MAKING TIME: 5½ hours

1. Make the strips of fringing to decorate the piñata with. Set aside one roll of the crepe paper for the swags (see steps 4–8). Take the remaining rolls of crepe paper out of the packaging but do not unfold it. Cut right across the crepe paper at 4 cm (1½ inch) intervals, almost as if slicing a leek or scallion; don't unroll the strips yet, but keep them as folded wads. To create the fringing, make 3 cm (1¼ inch) cuts into one long edge of each wad, spaced about 1 cm (⅜ inch) apart. You'll also need to slide the scissors into the centre of the wad and make an extra cut down each outside edge where the folded is, otherwise you'll end up with some of the fringing being unevenly spaced. Now unfold the paper, and you should have a long strip of evenly spaced fringing. Repeat this process for each wad.

2. Turn the 'cake' upside down and apply a line of glue around the edge of the circular base.

3. Glue a strip of crepe paper around the outside edge of the circular base, with the fringing hanging over the edge. Apply a line of glue 1 cm (⅜ inch) from the edge of the first strip, and then glue another crepe paper strip to this, making sure that the fringe overhangs the solid edge of the first strip, and that the overlap covers up any of the cardboard underneath. Continue adding successive strips, working your way into the centre in smaller circles until you have covered the whole base.

4. Turn the cake back over and start at the bottom edge, layering the crepe paper fringing as you move upward, with the uncut edge at the top of each row. Make sure to cover the flap too. Once the 'cake' has been covered completely with the fringing you can trim the edges and cut off any unruly pieces of fringe.

5. To make a swag decoration, cut a rectangular piece of crepe paper 23 x 40 cm (9 x 16 inches). Make the shorter cut across the grain of the crepe paper. Stretch this crepe paper out a little.

6. Scrunch up the long edge of the paper and glue to secure, then repeat on the other long edge. This should form a swag shape. Glue the swag to the uppermost edge of the bottom tier.

7. Repeat the above process until the edge is lined with swags. If any cut edges on the top or bottom of the swags are visible, simply tuck them under. You should require 9 swags for the bottom tier, 7 for the middle tier and 6 for the top tier.

8. To make a rosette, cut a 6 x 50 cm (2½ x 20 inch) strip of crepe paper, and gently stretch one edge of the paper, a few inches at a time, pulling on it while it gives easily, but stopping if it is in danger of tearing

9. Apply glue along the unstretched edge and curl the paper in on itself, scrunching the glued edge together so that it sticks. Glue the rosette in to the space between two swags.

10. Gently pull the folds of the unglued and previously stretched edge apart to form the rosette shape, so that it opens out to create a roselike effect. You will require nine rosettes for the bottom tier, seven for the middle tier and six for the top tier.

11. When the piñata is finished, check it over and remove any stray glue strings. If you have filled the piñata already, you can seal the flaps by gluing them down. If you are doing this nearer the time or at the venue itself, make sure you keep your glue gun handy!

CHAPTER FOUR

Home(spun) is where the heart is

Just two days before my wedding (which was to be held in April in the northern English town I grew up in) I was driving up the motorway with my future husband, on our way to prepare the venue, when the weather began to take a significant turn for the worse. We had planned a marquee wedding in my parents' garden and the storm threatened to put a dampener on the day, in more ways than one. I can still remember looking at my soon-to-be Mister and realising that I didn't care about the weather, it was just one day and I had the rest of my life with this lovely man.

In many ways, a wedding isn't about a big send-off: it's about the feeling of coming home. To celebrate that feeling, the cakes in this chapter have more of a vintage, homemade quality, while still tasting absolutely delicious.

THE CAKES

Wuthering Heights

CARROT CAKE

I have a good friend who dislikes any dried fruit, but I sneakily gave her some of this cake to sample and she loved it, even diving in for second helpings.

She did look very sheepish when I mentioned the fruit, but it didn't stop her from helping herself to another piece! The cake is decorated with real flowers, but you can use paper flowers to make the set-up easier for you if you prefer. I might even be tempted to find some lovely fresh carrots with their green fronds still attached and use those…

'WUTHERING HEIGHTS' AT A GLANCE

BAKING SKILL: EASY

DECORATING SKILL: EASY

HOW FAR IN ADVANCE CAN IT BE MADE?
Up to five days before the wedding. Fill the cake 24 hours before the wedding, then wrap the sides in plastic wrap. Alternatively, the layers of the cake can be baked and then frozen for up to three months. As soon as the cake has cooled, wrap each layer in plastic wrap and then foil. Be careful that each layer doesn't get squashed or bashed while it is in the freezer.

SETTING UP:
Give yourself an hour to set the cake out and add the flowers. This cake will keep fresh around six hours from unwrapping; any longer and the sides of the cake will start to dry out and the flowers will begin to wilt. If you are in a very warm, dry environment then it may be even sooner.

PORTIONS:
Each cake is made up of two layers and there are three cakes making up the whole, six layers in all. Each 20 cm (8 inch) cake yields 25 portions (75 portions in total).

PRICE PER PORTION: MEDIUM

TOTAL MAKING TIME:
5½ hours

TOTAL BAKING TIME:
4½ hours

CARROT CAKE RECIPE

PREP: 30 minutes per layer.

Ingredient quantities are for one layer: you will need six layers to recreate this cake. If you have multiple tins then you can bake up to three layers at once. You may have to switch them around after 30 minutes, to prevent overcooking where there may be a hotspot. Obviously you will need to double the ingredients for two tins' worth or triple them if you are making three layers at a time.

---

100 g (3½ oz) unsalted butter
100 g (3½ oz) light brown sugar
50 g (1¾ oz) dark brown sugar
3 eggs
1 teaspoon natural vanilla extract
150 g (5½ oz) self-raising flour
1 teaspoon ground cinnamon
1 teaspoon mixed (pumpkin pie) spice
½ teaspoon salt
200 g (7 oz) grated carrot
30 g (1 oz) walnut pieces
75 g (2¾ oz) sultanas (golden raisins)
grated zest of 1 orange

1. Preheat the oven to 180°C (350°F).

2. Grease and line a 20 cm (8 inch) cake tin(s).

3. Melt the butter and set aside to cool.

4. Using a standing electric mixer fitted with the whisk attachment, beat together the combined sugar with the eggs until the mixture is light and fluffy. It should take around 4 minutes and should double in size.

5. Fold in the cooled melted butter and vanilla extract until they are totally incorporated into the egg mixture.

6. Sift the flour, spices and salt together over the egg mixture and fold in gently. You need to keep as much air in the mixture as possible.

7. Fold in the grated carrot, walnuts, sultanas and orange zest.

8. Spoon the mixture into the tin. If you are baking more than one tin at a time then measure (or weigh) the mixture to divide it evenly between the tins. You want the baked layers to be as equal as possible to create a uniform cake.

9. Bake for 45 minutes: the cake is ready when a skewer inserted into the centre of the cake comes out clean.

BUTTERCREAM

PREP: 15 minutes per batch. To recreate the cake you will require three batches of the buttercream recipe below. If you have a standing electric mixer you could make it in two batches, but you will need to make it in three or even four batches if you are mixing the buttercream by hand. If you try to mix up a triple quantity with a handheld mixer you will more than likely burn out the motor.

450 g (1 lb) unsalted butter, softened
450 g (1 lb) icing (confectioners') sugar
grated zest of 2 lemons
3 tablespoons freshly squeezed lemon juice

1. Beat the butter until it is light and fluffy.

2. Add the icing sugar and lemon zest and beat together well for about 5 minutes. You should find that the colour of the buttercream will really lighten: it should change from yellow to almost white.

3. Add the lemon juice and beat in well.

LAYERING AND TIERING THE CAKE

PREP: 24 hours ahead, covering the drum, 10 minutes; 15 minutes per tier

EQUIPMENT
25 cm (10 inch) covered cake drum (see page 41)
25 cm (10 inch) thin cake board
two 18 cm (7 inch) thin cake boards
cake leveller or a large serrated knife and cocktail sticks (toothpicks)
palette knife (or alternative, see page 37)
spirit level (optional)

1. Level the layers using the method described on page 37. Brush off as many loose crumbs as you can from each layer.

2. Put a blob of buttercream on the 25 cm (10 inch) cake board then position one layer of the cake on top. Add a 2 cm (¾ inch) layer of buttercream, either with a palette knife, making sure that the layer of buttercream is even all over the top as any unevenness will cause the cake stack to topple. Or you can use a piping (icing) bag (cut a 2 cm (¾ inch) hole in a disposable bag) to pipe a layer of concentric circles that you then smooth over with a knife: this technique creates a more even layer.

3. Cut a strip of baking paper and wrap it around the side of the cake. You should find that the paper will stick to the buttercream, but if your buttercream proves particularly unsticky (or should that be stickless?) then secure the ends with some tape. Use a palette knife and spread the buttercream to the edge of the cake until it is flush to the paper. Do this to ensure a good clean edge to the buttercream so that your finished cake will look fabulous, darling!

>>

4. Remove the baking paper. Place the next layer on the buttercream layer and take a moment to line it up so that there are no overhanging edges. Use a spirit level on top of this layer: if it is not level, gently push down the side of the cake that is too high.

5. Add a layer of buttercream using the same method as in steps 2 and 3.

6. Transfer the cake to the covered cake board (if using one), and dowel using the method described on page 50.

7. Repeat with the remaining two tiers (four layers), placing each cake on one of the 18 cm (7 inch) boards.

8. The top layer of each cake should be covered with a layer of buttercream.

9. Stack the cakes using dowels, following the method described on page 50.

SPREAD THE BUTTERCREAM 3

DECORATING THE CAKE

PREP: 40 minutes to wire the flowers, 10 minutes to attach them to the cake

EQUIPMENT
2 large white roses or decorative white cabbages
5 freesia sprays
3 hydrangea or shamrock chrysanthemum heads
6 sprigs with a small yellow flower such as Astilbe
8 large sprigs of rosemary (if you have rosemary in your garden, use this as it will stay fresher for longer than the supermarket variety. Pick it on the morning of the wedding, or the evening before and stand in water overnight)
26-gauge florists' wire
18-gauge florists' wire
florists' tape
wire cutters (although you may get away with a pair of very strong kitchen scissors)

1. Wire the flowers using the method described on page 57, remembering to completely cover the ends of the stems, to give the flowers a longer shelf life and prevent any sap seeping into the cake. The rosemary does not need to be wired.

2. Place the cake on your cake stand (if using one). Add the sprigs of rosemary around the base of the cake.

3. Put the flowers on the cake, starting from the top and working down. Add the larger flowers first and then hide any visible wires with the smaller elements. Create a large bunch of flowers on one side of the cake with a smaller bunch at the base of the cake on the opposite side for a balanced look.

Five Gold Rings

BUNDT CAKES

While these delicious cakes are not true gold, they are worth their weight in the proverbial metal.

These cakes are really simple to make and an absolute doddle to decorate. The project is an easy one to adapt if you need more or fewer portion numbers (just make more or fewer cakes!) I'm envisioning a wedding in a village hall with tons of bunting and cups of tea in old china, so all of the recipes are based on classic tea-time treats, such as lemon drizzle, cherry bakewell, gingerbread and banana.

'FIVE GOLD RINGS' AT A GLANCE

BAKING SKILL: EASY

Although there are different flavours they are all versions of one bundt cake recipe. You can borrow tins from friends and family if you wish to show off different cake shapes; however, I have to admit I find it quite tricky to release the cakes from the traditional metal bundt pans without losing bits of the cake. So to make this project as easy as possible I would recommend the silicon bundt pans: there is no need for greasing them and the cake literally slides out completely intact, *et voilà*! If you do have a baking disaster and are faced with raggedy-edged cakes simply cover the offending area with more icing and no-one will be the wiser.

Use a 22 cm (8½ inch) diameter bundt tin with a 10 cm (4 inch) high side for each cake.

DECORATING SKILL: EASY

HOW FAR IN ADVANCE CAN IT BE MADE?

The cakes can be baked up to five days before the wedding, and iced up to four days before the big day (then they need to be stored in airtight containers). The decorations can be added when setting up. Alternatively, the cakes can be made up to three months in advance of the day and frozen. Leave them at room temperature to defrost completely before icing.

SETTING UP:

This shouldn't take any more than 20 minutes to set out. The cakes can be set up on the morning of the wedding, and will keep all day.

PORTIONS:

Each cake serves 20 portions.

PRICE PER PORTION: LOW

TOTAL MAKING TIME:

2½ hours

TOTAL BAKING TIME:

7½–9 hours

VANILLA BUNDT CAKE

PREP: 25 minutes

325 g (11½ oz) unsalted butter
500 g (1 lb 2 oz) caster (superfine) sugar
4 eggs
2½ teaspoons natural vanilla extract
500 g (1 lb 2 oz) self-raising flour
¼ teaspoon fine salt
285 ml (9¾ fl oz) buttermilk

GLAZE
50 g (1¾ oz) caster (superfine) sugar
50 ml (1¾ fl oz) water
1 teaspoon vanilla extract

ICING
100 g (3½ oz) icing (confectioners') sugar
1 teaspoon natural vanilla extract
2 teaspoons water

1. Preheat the oven to 170°C (325°F). If you are using a metal bundt tin, use a pastry brush to brush melted butter all over the tin; be sure to grease every nook and cranny. Shake a tablespoon of flour into the tin and tilt the tin until every part of the surface is covered with flour, then tip out any excess.

2. Beat the butter and sugar together until pale and fluffy: this should take 3–5 minutes.

3. Beat in the eggs one at a time.

4. Add the vanilla extract.

5. Beat in the flour and salt, taking care not to overbeat, then turn the mixer to a low setting and stop beating as soon as all the flour is incorporated.

6. Beat in the buttermilk, stopping as soon as it is incorporated into the mixture.

7. Spoon the batter into the tin. If you are using a silicone mould, stand it on a baking tray.

8. Bake for 1 hour 30 minutes to 1 hour 45 minutes: the cake is ready when a skewer inserted into the thickest part of the cake comes out clean.

9. Leave the cake in the tin to cool for 30 minutes then turn it out onto a wire rack. Stand the wire rack on a large baking tray (preferably one with a lip).

10. Make the glaze by heating the sugar and liquid ingredients in a pan. As soon as the syrup has come to a boil, remove the pan from the heat and pour the glaze all over the top of the cake. You will find some of it will run off (that's why you need the tray underneath), but don't worry, most of it will soak in, producing a lovely moist cake.

11. Beat the icing ingredients together, then drizzle the icing over the cake. You can use a piping (icing) bag if you have one; however, drizzling the icing from a spoon will also create a very pleasing effect (see page 165).

LEMON AND POPPY SEED BUNDT CAKE

PREP: 25 minutes

325 g (11½ oz) unsalted butter
500 g (1 lb 2 oz) caster (superfine) sugar
grated zest and juice of 2 lemons
4 eggs
500 g (1 lb 2 oz) self-raising flour
¼ teaspoon fine salt
285 ml (9¾ fl oz) buttermilk
2 tablespoons poppy seeds

GLAZE

50 ml (1¾ fl oz) lemon juice
50 g (1¾ oz) caster (superfine) sugar
pared peel of two lemons (see page 21)

ICING

100 g (3½ oz) icing (confectioners') sugar
15 ml (½ fl oz) lemon juice

Follow the directions for the vanilla bundt cake, with the following additions:

1. Add the lemon zest to the butter and sugar and beat together.

2. Add the lemon juice instead of the vanilla at step 4.

3. Mix in the poppy seeds after step 6.

4. Add the pared lemon peel to the lemon juice and sugar while making the glaze in step 10.

5. Strain the peel out of the glaze and reserve.

6. Sprinkle the peel over the top of the cake once it has been iced.

BANANA BUNDT CAKE

PREP: 25 minutes

325 g (11½ oz) unsalted butter
500 g (1 lb 2 oz) light brown sugar
4 eggs
3 ripe bananas, about 380 g (13½ oz) after peeling
2½ teaspoons natural vanilla extract
2 tablespoons ground cinnamon
500 g (1 lb 2 oz) self-raising flour
¼ teaspoon fine salt
285 ml (9¾ fl oz) buttermilk

GLAZE

50 ml (1¾ fl oz) water
50 g (1¾ oz) caster (superfine) sugar
1 teaspoon natural vanilla extract

ICING

100 g (3½ oz) icing (confectioners') sugar
15 ml (½ fl oz) lemon juice

Follow the directions for the vanilla bundt cake, with the following additions:

1. Mash the bananas and add them to the mix after the eggs at step 3.

2. Add the cinnamon with the flour in step 5.

CHERRY AND ALMOND BUNDT CAKE

PREP: 25 minutes

325 g (11½ oz) unsalted butter
500 g (1 lb 2 oz) caster (superfine) sugar
4 eggs
1 teaspoon almond essence
400 g (14 oz) self-raising flour
¼ teaspoon fine salt
125 g (4½ oz) ground almonds
285 ml (9¾ fl oz) buttermilk
150 g (5½ oz) glacé cherries

GLAZE
50 ml (1¾ fl oz) water
50 g (1¾ oz) caster (superfine) sugar
1 teaspoon natural vanilla extract

ICING
100 g (3½ oz) icing (confectioners') sugar
1 teaspoon almond essence
2 teaspoons water

DECORATION
12 whole glacé cherries, washed and dried

Follow the directions for the vanilla bundt cake, with the following additions:

1. Substitute the almond essence for the vanilla extract in step 4.

2. Add the ground almonds with the flour at step 5.

3. Wash and dry the cherries, cut them into quarters and fold them into the batter after the buttermilk has been incorporated.

4. Place the whole glacé cherries on the top of the cake once it has been iced.

DRIZZLE THE ICING

11

GINGERBREAD BUNDT CAKE

PREP: 25 minutes

325 g (11½ oz) unsalted butter
300 g (10½ oz) dark brown sugar
100 g (3½ oz) golden syrup (if you cannot find this,
   substitute an extra 100 g brown sugar)
100 g (3½ oz) treacle
4 eggs
500 g (1 lb 2 oz) self-raising flour
¼ teaspoon fine salt
1 teaspoon ground allspice
1 tablespoon ground ginger
1 tablespoon ground cinnamon
5 cm (2 inch) piece of fresh ginger
285 ml (9¾ fl oz) buttermilk

GLAZE
90 g (3¼ oz) golden syrup (if you can't find golden syrup,
   make a sugar syrup with 30 g (1 oz) of brown sugar and
   30 ml (1 fl oz) water)

ICING
100 g (3½ oz) icing (confectioners') sugar
15 ml (½ fl oz) lemon juice

DECORATION
50 g (1¾ oz) crystallised ginger, cut into small chunks

Follow the directions for the vanilla bundt cake, with the following additions:

1. Add the syrup and treacle with the sugar to the butter in step 2.

2. Add the spices to the flour and mix them into the batter at step 5, then grate in the fresh ginger using a microplane and mix it in well.

3. Heat the golden syrup in a pan to use as the glaze.

4. Sprinkle the crystallised ginger over the top of the cake once it has been iced.

DECORATING THE CAKE

CRAFTING TIME: 30 minutes

EQUIPMENT
6 A4 (Letter) sheets of craft paper
templates (see page 226)
scissors (alternatively, you could use three different-size heart
*   craft punches)*
bamboo skewers
cocktail sticks (toothpicks)
glue stick

1. To make each topper you will need to cut out three heart shapes of the same size. Use the template as a guide, or a craft punch.

2. Fold each heart in half.

3. Apply glue to half of the back of one heart, and stick it to the back of another heart, as if you were gluing them together back to back.

4. Apply glue to the back of the third heart, and glue this between the other two, so that each heart is stuck to each of the others to form a three-dimensional shape. When assembled you should have a shape that is reminiscent of an upside-down arrow tip.

5. Push a skewer or cocktail stick into the pointy end of the formed shape.

6. Create a variety of these hearts of different sizes and on different lengths of sticks. You can cut some of the skewers down to create different lengths.

7. Push the skewers or cocktail sticks into the cakes.

To create the cakes pictured you'll need 8 large hearts, 6 medium hearts and 4 mini ones.

PAPER HEARTS 6

The Bee's Knees

HONEY CAKE

Surely there can be nothing that better represents all the great qualities of home produce than a dripping pot of fragrant honey.

From its origin in a garden filled with delightfully buzzing bees, by way of a mysterious and magical process, you are provided with a hive full of the sweetest honey. My soundtrack for the summer is the hum of bees as they steal pollen from my garden, so I have stolen some back from them to create this recipe for you: summer in cake form.

'THE BEE'S KNEES' AT A GLANCE

BAKING SKILL: MEDIUM

Although a relatively easy batter to mix up, baking a cake in one tin rather than three can cause issues, so you need to be sure that the cake is cooked all the way through without being overcooked and dry on the outside.

DECORATING SKILL: MEDIUM

You will need some rudimentary sewing skills.

HOW FAR IN ADVANCE CAN IT BE MADE?

These cakes can be baked up to five days in advance and covered up to four days in advance. They can also be baked three months in advance and frozen. Defrost thoroughly before covering with marzipan.

SETTING UP:

This shouldn't take any more than half an hour to set out. These cakes can be set up the day before the event, as long as it is a stable environment with no swings of temperature. High humidity can also be an issue, causing the fondant to sweat and mark the ribbon.

PORTIONS:

15 cm (6 inch), 14 portions;
20 cm (8 inch), 25 portions;
25 cm (10 inch), 45 portions.

PRICE PER PORTION: LOW

TOTAL MAKING TIME:

6 hours plus 12 hours drying time.

TOTAL BAKING TIME:

Maximum of 6½ hours.

CAKE RECIPE

PREP: Each cake will take 20–30 minutes to prepare. You can mix up all three tiers at once and bake them together in the oven, but you will need a standing electric mixer to do this, as a hand whisk won't cope with that much batter.

15 CM (6 INCH) CAKE: bake for 1 hour 45 minutes

175 g (6 oz) butter
200 g (7 oz) lavender sugar (see note)
100 g (3½ oz) honey
3 eggs
350 g (12 oz) self-raising flour
100 ml (3½ fl oz) buttermilk
1 teaspoon reserved lavender flowers (optional)

20 CM (8 INCH) CAKE: bake for 2 hours

300 g (10½ oz) butter
350 g (12 oz) lavender sugar (see note)
175 g (6 oz) honey
5 eggs
575 g (1 lb 4½ oz) self-raising flour
175 ml (5½ fl oz/⅔ cup) buttermilk
2 teaspoons reserved lavender flowers (optional)

25 CM (10 INCH) CAKE: bake for 2¾ hours

425 g (15 oz) butter
475 g (1 lb ¾ oz) lavender sugar (see note)
225 g (8 oz) honey
7 eggs
825 g (1 lb 13 oz) self-raising flour
275 ml (9½ fl oz) buttermilk
4 teaspoons reserved lavender flowers (optional)

1. Preheat the oven to 160°C (315°F). Grease and line the cake tin(s) with two layers of baking paper.

2. Beat the butter and sugar together until much paler and fluffier: this should take 3–5 minutes.

3. Beat in the honey.

4. Add the eggs one at a time and beat in well. If the mixture curdles, then add a tablespoon of flour.

5. Fold in the flour and buttermilk, alternating half of each at a time and making sure each addition is totally incorporated into the mixture before adding any more. If you are using lavender flowers, fold them in now.

6. Spoon the batter into the tin(s); if you have baking strips, place these around the tin(s), or use an alternative (see page 26). Bake for the required time, but do check the cake(s) about 15 minutes before they should be ready to make sure they don't overcook. The cake(s) are ready when the top is springy to the touch and a skewer inserted into the middle comes out clean.

7. Leave the cake(s) to cool for 15 minutes in the tin(s) and then turn out onto a wire rack to cool completely.

Note   *Two weeks before you bake the cakes, mix 1 kg (2 lb 4 oz) of unrefined caster (superfine) sugar with 3 tablespoons of lavender flowers. You can buy edible lavender or use lavender from your own garden (if it has been grown without pesticides). Be aware that not all types of lavender are edible, so check before you use it. Keep the sugar in an airtight container until you need it. Then sift the sugar to remove the lavender flowers just before baking. Reserve the sifted lavender flowers.*

COVERING THE CAKES

PREP: 24 hours ahead, covering the drum, 10 minutes;
30–40 minutes per cake plus 12 hours drying out time for the marzipan

EQUIPMENT
rolling pin
spacers (optional)
smoothers (optional)
sharp knife
30 cm (12 inch) covered cake drum (see page 41)
30 cm (12 inch) cake board
25 cm (10 inch) cake board
two 20 cm (8 inch) thin cake boards
15 cm (6 inch) thin cake board
140 ml (4⅝ oz) honey, warmed

MARZIPAN
15 cm (6 inch), 600 g (1 lb 5 oz); 20 cm (8 inch), 1 kg
  (2 lb 4 oz); 25 cm (10 inch), 1.45 kg (3 lb 3½ oz)

FONDANT
15 cm (6 inch), 600 g (1 lb 5 oz); 20 cm (8 inch), 800 g
  (1 lb 12 oz); 25 cm (10 inch), 1.25 kg (2 lb 12 oz)

1. Cover the cakes with marzipan using the method described on page 46, using honey instead of the sugar syrup. When covering the 25 cm (10 inch) cake, place it on the spare 30 cm (12 inch) board. Once it has been covered with the fondant you can transfer it to the covered cake drum. Remember to stand the smaller cakes on the thin cake boards before covering them.

2. Leave the marzipan to harden for a day, then slightly dampen the surface with water and cover the cakes with fondant using the method described on page 49.

ASSEMBLING THE TIERS

PREP: 10–15 minutes

Use the method described on page 50 to dowel and assemble the tiers.

DECORATING THE CAKE

CRAFTING TIME: 2 hours 30 minutes

EQUIPMENT

white fabric
white sewing thread
scissors
needle and pins
variety of floral print fabrics, lace and ribbons that match
your colour scheme
iron and ironing board
template (see page 226)
kitchen string
60 cm (24 inches) narrow ribbon
paper straws

Wash, dry and iron the plain white fabric before you start sewing, to ensure that it has no starch or chemicals on it that may contaminate your cake.

SEW THE COLLARS

6

15 CM (6 INCH) CAKE

1. Cut out a 9 cm (3½ inch) wide strip of the plain white fabric that measures 54 cm (21½ inches) long.

2. Remove any loose threads and iron it flat.

3. Fold a 5 mm (¼ inch) double hem (so that no raw edges are showing) on each of the short edges, iron the hems flat and sew them down using a simple running stitch.

4. Choose the lace or fabric that you wish to use on this strip, and cut it slightly longer than needed. If you are using fabric, do not worry about frayed edges, as this will add to the charm of the piece, but do make sure that it is cut relatively straight.

5. Lay the embellishments on to the white fabric strip in the desired order. Pin them down.

6. Use a small running stitch to sew the pieces together. Try to use tiny stiches on the front of the fabric; if you are using a piece of lace that has a very scalloped edge make sure to sew down the tops of the scallops so that they don't flop down once it's on the cake.

7. When all the pieces are sewn down, trim the edges straight if necessary.

8. Sew a 20 cm (8 inch) length of narrow ribbon or lace at the middle of each of the short ends of the collar.

9. Press the collar flat (make sure the iron isn't too hot or you may melt any polyester lace or ribbon).

20 CM (8 INCH) CAKE

1. Cut out a 9 cm (3½ inch) wide strip of the plain white fabric that measures 70.5 cm (27¾ inches) long.

2. Repeat steps 2–9 (see page 173) to create the collar for the middle tier.

25 CM (10 INCH) CAKE

1. Cut out a 9 cm (3½ inch) wide strip of the plain white fabric that measures 85 cm (33½ inches) long.

2. Repeat the previous steps 2–9 (see page 173) to create the collar for the lower tier.

BUNTING

1. Use the template to cut out 8 tiny flags in the same fabrics that you have used for the collars.

2. Turn the top of each flag over by 7 mm (⅜ inch). Iron it flat.

3. Lay the flags down on a work surface in the order that you want them to be on the kitchen string.

4. Fold a 69 cm (27 inch) length of kitchen string in half to find the middle. Sew the first flag immediately to one side of the middle, laying the twine under the fold at the top of the flag before you start to sew with running stitch. Sew the three next flags, make a knot and cut the thread.

5. Go back to the centre and sew the four flags on the other side of the middle point.

6. Tie each end of the bunting to the top of a paper straw. Trim off any excess twine.

FINAL TOUCHES

Place the cake on a cake stand (if you are using one). Once the cake is in situ, insert the straws into the top tier of the cake, and tie the collars around each layer using the ribbons, positioning the ties out of sight at the back of the cake.

Love-in-a-box

SHORTBREAD, ICED GEMS & MELTING MOMENTS

My Irish family love a celebration almost as much as they love a biscuit with their tea, and at most weddings tea and biscuits are an integral part of the day.

Apparently, in parts of Scotland, it was tradition to break a piece of shortbread over the head of the bride: I'm not sure if this was meant to be symbolic of good fortune or just to provide entertainment for the guests, and I certainly won't advocate this custom unless you want an angry bride! Also, it sounds like a waste of good shortbread...

'LOVE-IN-A-BOX' AT A GLANCE

BAKING SKILL: EASY

DECORATING SKILL: EASY

As a nod towards a more orthodox wedding cake, I have suggested that you present the biscuits stacked in tiers of tins. Because the biscuits are safely stored away, you don't need to worry about any flowers you may wish to display on the top. If you are hiring a florist you can ask them to make an extra posy of flowers to place on the 'cake', or pick a bunch of flowers from your garden and display them in a vintage cup and saucer.

If you have any difficulty sourcing a set of tins that will match your colour scheme then you can spray them with paint. The tins I bought for this project included lettering on the lids that I didn't like, so I sprayed the lids plain cream. (Do use a mask if you are spraying paint, and always work outside with plenty of paper as the spray will go everywhere and leave permanent marks.) Most craft shops will stock a suitable paint.

I used 18 cm (7 inch), 23 cm (9 inch) and 25 cm (10 inch) biscuit tins. If you are using different sizes you may need to change the quantities or the size of the shortbread.

HOW FAR IN ADVANCE CAN IT BE MADE?

All of the biscuits can be made and decorated up to two weeks before the wedding and stored in their tins. The biscuits dough can also be made up to three months in advance of the wedding and frozen.

SETTING UP:

You'll need just a few minutes to set the tins out. The tins can be stacked in place at any time prior to the wedding. If you are creating a floral display yourself, then do this on the morning of the big day.

PORTIONS:

Shortbread, 36 pieces; melting moments, 40 biscuits; iced gems, 40 (allowing for four of the mini biscuits per person)

PRICE PER PORTION: LOW

TOTAL MAKING TIME:

3 hours 20 minutes

TOTAL BAKING TIME:

2 hours (assuming you have large baking trays).

ON THE DAY:

Transport the biscuits in the tins and stack them up on the display table. Add a prepared posy on top, or fill a teacup with garden flowers for a more homespun look.

SHORTBREAD

PREP: 20 minutes;
BAKING TIME: 35–40 minutes

120 g (4¼ oz) icing (confectioners') sugar
240 g (8¾ oz) plain (all-purpose) flour
120 g (4¼ oz) rice flour (or fine polenta)
240 g (8¾ oz) unsalted butter, at room temperature,
  cut into small squares

1. Preheat the oven to 150°C (300°F). Line 2 large baking trays with baking paper.

2. Sift the icing sugar and combined flours into a bowl. (If you are using polenta, just add this straight to the bowl.) Add the butter.

3. Rub the butter into the dry ingredients using your fingertips. Keep rubbing until all of the ingredients are incorporated and the mixture forms a dough.

4. Briefly knead the dough on the work surface, but be careful not to overwork it or the shortbread will become tough. Lightly flour the surface if you find the dough is sticking.

5. Cut out a 15 cm (6 inch) diameter circle from baking paper. This will fit an 18 cm (7 inch) cake tin. If using a different size tin, cut the circle a little smaller than the tin's diameter.

6. Divide the dough into 6 equal portions: you may find it helpful to weigh them to get the division exact.

7. Lightly flour the work surface and roll out one of the portions of dough until it is just slightly bigger than the paper template. Cut out the dough using the template to create a 15 cm (6 inch) circle. Lay the circle on a baking tray.

8. Use the back of a dessert spoon pressed around the edge of the circle to create a pattern. Then, using a sharp knife, score the dough to create 6 wedges. Use a fork to add more pattern to the dough.

9. Roll out and shape the remaining balls of dough using the process described above. Put the baking trays in the oven and cook for 35–40 minutes until the dough feels firm and the edges of each circle are golden brown. (You may need to turn the trays around halfway through the baking process to prevent burning.)

10. Leave the shortbread to cool on the baking trays. If the decoration on the shortbread has lost its definition during baking then press lightly over the score marks with the side of a palette knife, but do be careful not to press too hard or you may break the biscuits.

11. Store the cooled shortbread in the 18 cm (7 inch) biscuit tin.

ADD A PATTERN

8

MELTING MOMENTS

PREP: 30 minutes;
BAKING TIME: 12 minutes per tray

---

225 g (8 oz) butter
175 g (6 oz) caster (superfine) sugar
2 tablespoons golden syrup (if you can't find golden syrup,
*   use corn or glucose syrup)*
100 g (3½ oz) rolled oats
225 g (8 oz) plain (all-purpose) flour

1. Preheat the oven to 180°C (350°F).

2. Beat the butter and caster sugar together until just mixed.

3. Add the syrup, oats and flour and stir until everything is combined.

4. Roll into forty 25 g (1 oz) balls. Set out the balls on a baking tray lined with baking paper. Space them 10 cm (4 inches) apart, as they will spread.

5. Bake for 12 minutes until golden brown around the edges. Leave to cool on the tray for 5 minutes then transfer to a wire rack to cool completely.

6. Store the biscuits in an airtight container until you are ready to decorate them.

DECORATIONS
PREP: 10 minutes
ICING TIME: 20 minutes

12 g (⁷⁄₁₆ oz) powdered egg white
500 g (1 lb 2 oz) icing (confectioners') sugar
80 ml (2½ fl oz/⅓ cup) water
3 tablespoons lemon juice
20 glacé cherries, washed, dried and halved

1. Put the powdered egg white and icing sugar in a bowl and mix them together well.

2. Gradually add the water and beat until the icing has reached a stiff peak consistency.

3. Add the lemon juice, a spoonful at a time, beating until the consistency of the icing is similar to thick (double) cream.

4. Drop a teaspoonful of icing onto the centre of each biscuit (the icing should spread out but not be too runny). Place a cherry half in the middle of the pool of icing, cut side down.

5. Leave the biscuits overnight for the icing to harden, then store them in the 23 cm (9 inch) tin.

ICED GEMS

PREP: 1 hour 20 minutes, plus overnight chilling;
BAKING TIME: 15 minutes per tray

225 g (8 oz) unsalted butter
200 g (7 oz) caster (superfine) sugar
1 egg
1 teaspoon natural vanilla extract
375 g (13 oz) plain (all-purpose) flour

1. Beat together the butter and sugar until just combined.

2. Add the egg and vanilla extract and beat the mixture again.

3. Add the flour. Stop mixing as soon as the dough has come together.

4. Take the dough out of the bowl and pat it into a flattened cake shape.

5. Wrap the dough in plastic wrap and chill in the refrigerator for at least an hour, but preferably overnight.

6. Preheat the oven to 190°C (375°F). Line 2 large baking trays with baking paper.

7. Roll out the dough using 5 mm (¼ inch) spacers: if you don't have spacers then make sure all the dough is an even height.

8. Cut out circles using a 1.5 cm (⅝ inch) round cutter. Set the circles on the baking trays, leaving at least 2 cm (¾ inch) between them.

9. Bake for 12–15 minutes until the biscuits are firm to the touch and pale golden brown around the edges.

10. Allow to cool on the tray for a couple of minutes and then transfer to a wire rack to cool completely. Store the biscuits in an airtight container until required for decoration. »

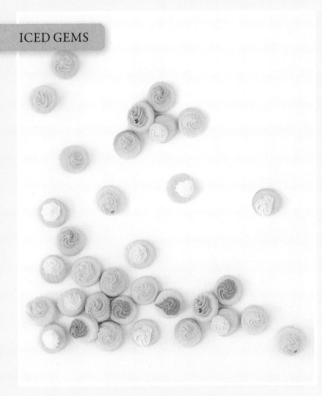

ICED GEMS

ICING SWIRLS

PREP: 20 minutes
ICING TIME: 30 minutes

12 g (⁷⁄₁₆ oz) powdered egg white
500 g (1 lb 2 oz) icing (confectioners') sugar
80 ml (2½ fl oz/⅓ cup) water
food colouring: yellow, orange, pink, purple

1. Put the powdered egg white and icing sugar in a bowl and mix together well.

2. Gradually add the water and beat until the icing has reached stiff peak consistency.

3. Divide the icing into 6 containers: leave one batch white and colour the others yellow, orange, pale pink, dark pink and purple. Add the food colouring one small drop at a time until you achieve the desired colour. Cover each container with plastic wrap until required.

4. Fit a piping (icing) bag and nozzle with a small star tip (a Wilton #13 would be perfect). Fill the bag with the white icing.

5. Hold a biscuit in one hand and hold the bag with the tip 5 mm (¼ inch) above the biscuit.

6. Squeeze the bag gently and make a circular motion with your wrist to form a swirled star.

7. Release the pressure on the bag and pull the bag away from the biscuit.

8. Continue in this manner until you have used all the white icing. Set out the iced biscuits on a tray for the icing to harden (preferably they should be left overnight, so that they don't get squished in the tin).

9. Put the yellow icing in the bag. The first few biscuits will have a two-tone swirl but this is deliberate. Ice the biscuits as before.

10. Continue in the same manner with each icing colour. You may have more icing than you need, so separate the biscuits into six equal piles before you start icing. If you have excess icing in the bag after finishing a pile then squeeze the excess out before adding the next colour.

11. Leave the biscuits overnight for the icing to harden, then store them in the tin.

APPLY THE SWIRLS

10

 Magic in the air

This is a section for the more unconventional amongst you: the bohemians and the ethereal, the wanderers and the artists, the mystics. So for this chapter try to imagine the wedding of Titania and Oberon, the king and queen of the fairies, wandering through a beautiful wood along with their entourages, delicate flowers entwined in their hair and magic being woven wherever they tread. I love being a part of the wedding industry and it is a real pleasure to be involved in some amazing weddings; I particularly love woodland or outdoor weddings. They do have a unique magical quality to them. I realise that there are some parts of the world (my own included) where it is quite a big gamble to plan an alfresco wedding; however, if you are all snug in a teepee tent, even if it's raining you will still feel part of the great outdoors. You can bring some artistry and magic to your day with these cake projects and weave your own magic on your guests.

The Cakes

Lulled in these Flowers

ELDERFLOWER & GOOSEBERRY CAKE

Imagine a beautifully scented bower, filled with precious wild flowers, each one shining like a tiny jewel ready to be plucked by the fairy queen.

Breathe in the perfumed air and be transported to a magical place. This cake will create a little piece of Titania's floral dream for your wedding day. Elderflowers have a distinctive musky perfume and they are most often found in a country hedgerow, filling the surrounding lanes with their fabulous aroma (you can find them flowering in early summer).

'LULLED IN THESE FLOWERS' AT A GLANCE

BAKING SKILL: EASY

I have included a recipe for elderflower cordial; however, don't despair if you feel that making your own cordial is too much. Most supermarkets now stock different varieties of this heavenly nectar (and if you find it impossible to source it then substitute rose or orange blossom water and you can still create a floral-scented cake). Make sure to buy the cordial rather than a presse. The flavour pairing of elderflower and gooseberry is an exceptionally pleasant one: these two ingredients seem like a marriage made in heaven (particularly apt for this project).

DECORATING SKILL: EASY

This cake is decorated with everyday garden flowers, as they often possess a fragile and ethereal beauty; however, they do have a very short shelf life, especially in a warm environment, so I have crystallised the blooms. Otherwise they can wilt and the petals will curl up within only a couple of hours. Of course, if you prefer not to use crystallised flowers, you can use larger more robust flowers such as roses, which will hold their shape longer, especially if you wire them (see page 57 for advice on using flowers).

HOW FAR IN ADVANCE CAN IT BE MADE?

Up to five days before being served. The separate layers of the cake can be baked and then frozen up to three months before the big day. As soon as the cake has cooled wrap each layer in plastic wrap and then foil. Be careful that each layer doesn't get squashed or bashed while it is in the freezer. The cake can be layered, filled and tiered up to four days in advance. The decoration should be done on the day of the event.

The elderflower syrup should last for six months in a freezer.

The crystallised flowers will last up to six months, but do keep checking them over that time to make sure they are still perfect.

SETTING UP:

Give yourself an hour to set up and decorate the cake. This cake will last all day once set up, depending on the temperature of your venue.

PORTIONS:

Each tier is made up of three layers and two tiers make up the whole, so you will need six layers.
15 cm (6 inch), 14 portions;
20 cm (8 inch), 25 portions.

PRICE PER PORTION: LOW

TOTAL MAKING TIME:

8½ hours plus 24 hours steeping time and 3½ hours chilling and drying

TOTAL BAKING TIME:

3 hours

ELDERFLOWER CORDIAL

PREP: 20 minutes (plus time to pick the flowers), 24 hours steeping time, 20 minutes to drain

5 heads of elderflower (it is best to pick the flowers first thing on a dry sunny morning)
300 ml (10½ fl oz) water
450 g (1 lb) sugar
1 lemon

1. Give the elderflowers a good shake to make sure there are no insects hiding in them. Gently wash the flowers. Take off the larger stems: you don't need to pick every single flower, but the more stems you can get rid of the better. Put the flowers in a large bowl.

2. Put the water in a saucepan and pour in the sugar. Bring the mixture to a boil without stirring; you can swirl the water a few times if you wish to mix the ingredients together.

3. Zest the lemon (if you have a vegetable peeler, use that rather than a grater). Add the zest to the elderflowers, then slice the lemon and add the slices too.

4. When the syrup has boiled, pour it over the flowers and lemons. Cover the bowl and leave for 24 hours.

5. Strain the syrup through muslin (cheesecloth), or a clean tea towel (dish towel) will also do the job. The best way to do this is to turn a stool or a chair upside down. Place a bowl on the underside of the seat (which is now uppermost) and tie the corners of the cloth to the four legs of the stool. Pour the elderflower mixture through the cloth.

6. Pour the syrup into freezerproof containers and freeze until needed.

STEEP THE SYRUP

4

CAKE RECIPE

PREP: 20 minutes per layer; each tier is made up of three layers. Ingredients quantities are for one layer.
BAKING: 25–30 minutes per layer

---

15 CM (6 INCH) CAKE LAYER

100 g (3½ oz) unsalted butter, at room temperature
100 g (3½ oz) caster (superfine) sugar
2 large eggs, at room temperature
100 g (3½ oz) self-raising flour
2 tablespoons elderflower cordial

20 CM (8 INCH) CAKE LAYER

150 g (5½ oz) unsalted butter, at room temperature
150 g (5½ oz) caster (superfine) sugar
3 large eggs, at room temperature
150 g (5½ oz) self-raising flour
3 tablespoons elderflower cordial

1. Preheat the oven to 200°C (400°F).

2. Grease and line the sponge tin(s).

3. Beat the butter and sugar together until they are creamed. Add the eggs one by one (if the mixture curdles, add a teaspoon of flour).

4. Sift the flour into the bowl and fold it into the mixture with a spoon or spatula. Fold in the elderflower cordial.

5. Spoon the mixture into the prepared sponge tin and bake for 25–30 minutes, until a skewer inserted into the centre of the cake comes out clean. Leave the cake to cool in the tin for 10 minutes, then turn out onto a wire rack to cool completely.

BUTTERCREAM

PREP: 10 minutes per batch

---

15 CM (6 INCH) CAKE

500 g (1 lb 2 oz) unsalted butter, at room temperature
500 g (1 lb 2 oz) icing (confectioners') sugar
2 tablespoons elderflower cordial

20 CM (8 INCH) CAKE

650 g (1 lb 7 oz) unsalted butter, at room temperature
650 g (1 lb 7 oz) icing (confectioners') sugar
3 tablespoons elderflower cordial

1. Beat the butter until it is pale and fluffy.

2. Add the icing sugar and elderflower cordial and beat well.

LAYERING AND TIERING THE CAKE

PREP: 24 hours ahead, covering the drum, 10 minutes; 15–20 minutes per tier plus 20–30 minutes chilling time

EQUIPMENT

25 cm (10 inch) and 20 cm (8 inch) cake boards, uncovered
25 cm (10 inch) covered cake drum (see page 41)
15 cm (6 inch) thin cake board
cake leveller or a large serrated knife and cocktail sticks
  (toothpicks)
palette knife (or alternative, see page 37)
cake scraper (or alternative, see page 37)
spirit level (optional)
5 tablespoons gooseberry jam (3 for the 20 cm cake and 2 for
  the 15 cm cake)
3 tablespoons elderflower cordial

1. Level the layers using the method described on page 37. Warm the elderflower cordial and brush the top of each layer with the cordial. Fill the cake using the method described on page 42. One layer will be gooseberry jam and the second layer will have a 1 cm (⅜ inch) deep layer of buttercream. Remember to place the bottom layer of the small tier on the thin cake board before you start filling.

2. Crumb-coat each cake using the method described on page 45 and refrigerate for 20–30 minutes, until the buttercream has hardened.

COVERING THE CAKE

PREP: 5–10 minutes per tier

Add a thick layer of the buttercream to each cake. You will not need to layer as much on the top of the cake as on the sides, or the frosting may start to bulge up once you have merged the tiers, so add just enough to cover the crumb-coat and enable you to incorporate some texture. Spend a little time achieving a balanced texture around the cake using the palette knife. Remember that you are not trying to achieve a perfect finish. We're aiming for a more 'rustic' appearance.

Keep a few tablespoons of each of the buttercream batches to one side for any touch-ups needed after merging the tiers.

MERGING THE TIERS

PREP: 10 minutes

Place the cake on the covered cake drum (optional). Dowel the 20 cm (8 inch) tier using the method described on page 50, then place the 15 cm (6 inch) tier on top. Store in a cool dry environment (this cake can be stored in a refrigerator if it is particularly hot).

CRYSTALLISED FLOWERS

PREP: 1¼ hours for 50 flowers

----

about 50 flowers, such as pansies, primroses and six or seven
sprigs of flowering rosemary (you could even use some
elderflowers)
2 egg whites (use pasteurised)
100 g (3½ oz) caster (superfine) sugar
medium paintbrush
wire rack
paper towel

1. See page 57 for advice on edible flowers. If you are
    using flowers from your garden, then pick the flowers
    just before you crystallise them, making sure that you
    choose perfect flowers at the peak of their bloom. Leave
    some stem attached, as this will make it easier for you
    to handle the flowers while you crystallise them. Wash
    them gently then blot away the water with paper towel
    until completely dry.

2. Paint the front and back of each flower with egg white.
    Make sure that you cover every tiny bit of the surface
    with the egg white, as any part left unpainted will spoil.

3. Shake caster sugar over the flower, front and back.

4. If you spot any areas where the sugar has not stuck,
    paint over it again with a little of the egg white and
    shake over more caster sugar.

5. Gently shake off any excess sugar and lay the flower
    on top of the wire rack with the stem hanging through
    the gaps.

6. For the rosemary sprigs, paint them all over with the
    egg white, make sure you get into every nook and
    cranny. Then cover with sugar as before. The flowers
    should be dry in around 2 hours, but it would be best
    to leave them overnight.

7. Trim off any excess stems.

8. Store the flowers in a cardboard box lined with paper
    towel until needed, keeping the box in a cool dry place.

SUGAR-COATING REAL FLOWERS

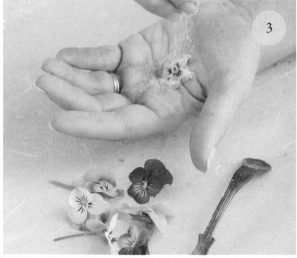

DECORATING THE CAKE

PREP: 20 minutes

Place the cake on a cake stand (if you are using one) prior to adding the flowers. You should find that the flowers will stick fairly easily to the buttercream, but do not press too hard as they are quite fragile and may break. Place the rosemary springs on the cake first, trimming any that are too long. Then add the flowers: don't space them too evenly around the cake, rather place them in clumps. Break off a few of the rosemary flowers and scatter them around.

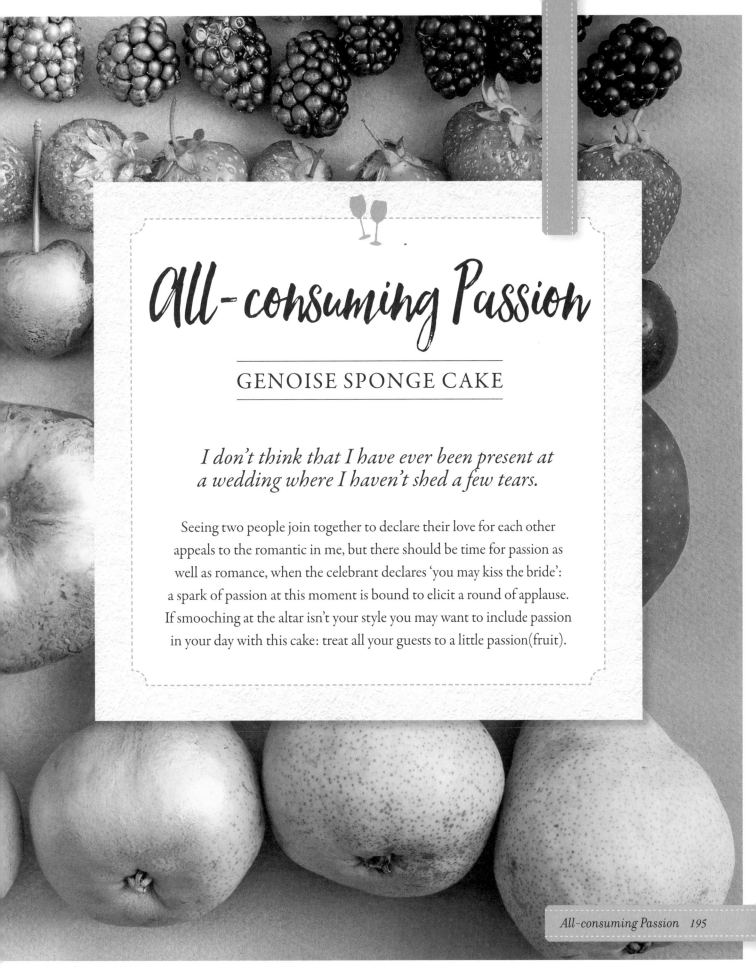

All-consuming Passion

GENOISE SPONGE CAKE

I don't think that I have ever been present at a wedding where I haven't shed a few tears.

Seeing two people join together to declare their love for each other appeals to the romantic in me, but there should be time for passion as well as romance, when the celebrant declares 'you may kiss the bride': a spark of passion at this moment is bound to elicit a round of applause. If smooching at the altar isn't your style you may want to include passion in your day with this cake: treat all your guests to a little passion(fruit).

'ALL-CONSUMING PASSION' AT A GLANCE

BAKING SKILL: HARD

The cake is a genoise sponge recipe, which is more complicated than a normal Victoria sponge, and the buttercream is a Swiss meringue recipe, which again needs more skill and experience than traditional buttercreams.

DECORATING SKILL: EASY

The buttercream frosting is very easy to apply and, if you can wield a spray can, the decorated fruit is a cinch!

You can tier this cake in the traditional way (see page 50 for details on how to achieve that); however, I think displaying each tier on a separate stand, each with its own golden crown of fruit, offers a much more striking effect.

HOW FAR IN ADVANCE CAN IT BE MADE?

The cake layers can be baked up to five days before the wedding, and filled and covered up to four days before the big day. Alternatively, the cake layers can be made up to three months in advance of the day and frozen. Leave them at room temperature to defrost completely before filling with the buttercream.

SETTING UP:

The cakes can be set up the night before the wedding and any hard fruit used for decoration placed on top. It will take you about half an hour. Any soft fruit such as berries or currants can be sprayed with the gold paint and stored in the fridge overnight, then added to the cake on the wedding morning. Do be aware that extreme temperatures may affect the buttercream covering and the soft fruit, in which case you may need to use under-ripe fruit to prevent this from happening.

PORTIONS:

12.5 cm (5 inch), 11 portions;
18 cm (7 inch), 20 portions;
23 cm (9 inch), 33 portions.

PRICE PER PORTION: HIGH

TOTAL MAKING TIME:

4 hours plus 2 hours for chilling and drying.

TOTAL BAKING TIME:

Up to 3 hours.

GENOISE SPONGE CAKE

PREP: 20 minutes per cake

12.5 CM (5 INCH) CAKE: bake for 45–55 minutes
50 g (1¾ oz) butter
3 eggs
125 g (4½ oz) caster (superfine) sugar
125 g (4½ oz) plain (all-purpose) flour
grated zest of 1 lemon

18 CM (7 INCH) CAKE: bake for 45–55 minutes
80 g (2¾ oz) butter
5 eggs
200 g (7 oz) caster (superfine) sugar
200 g (7 oz) plain (all-purpose) flour
grated zest of 1 lemon

23 CM (9 INCH) CAKE: bake for 60–70 minutes
130 g (4⅝ oz) butter
8 eggs
325 g (11½ oz) caster (superfine) sugar
325 g (11½ oz) plain (all-purpose) flour
grated zest of 2 lemons

1. Preheat the oven to 190°C (375°F). Grease and line the tin(s).

2. Melt the butter and leave it to cool.

3. Fill a large saucepan one-third full of water and bring it to the boil.

4. Put the eggs and sugar in a large heatproof bowl that fits snugly into the saucepan without the bottom of the bowl touching the water (the mixture will dramatically increase in size, so do make sure that you are using a large bowl). Once the water has boiled, remove the saucepan from the heat and set the bowl on top. Whisk the sugar and eggs together for 10 minutes. The mixture should approximately triple in quantity and become very pale and fluffy. After 10 minutes it should have reached the 'ribbon stage': if you lift the beaters out of the bowl a ribbon of the mixture should form that should take 3–4 seconds to disappear back into the batter.

5. Sift half the flour over the top of the egg mixture, fold it in very gently with a figure-of-eight movement using a large slotted spoon or a spatula. You don't want to lose any of the air that you have beaten in to the batter, but you must make sure that all of the flour is incorporated. Sift and fold in the remaining flour.

6. Slowly pour the butter into the mix and fold it in very gently. Fold in the lemon zest.

7. Pour the batter into the prepared tin(s).

8. Bake for 45–70 minutes (depending on the size of the cake) until the top is firm but springy to the touch and a skewer inserted into the middle comes out clean. Leave in the tin to cool slightly for 5 minutes, then turn out onto a wire rack to cool completely.

PASSIONFRUIT BUTTERCREAM

PREP: 30 minutes per batch

12.5 CM (5 INCH) CAKE

60 ml (2 fl oz/¼ cup) passionfruit juice (approximately
  3 passionfruit)
3 egg whites (use pasteurised)
200 g (7 oz) caster (superfine) sugar
325 g (11½ oz) unsalted butter, at room temperature
orange food colouring
1 teaspoon passionfruit seeds

18 CM (7 INCH) CAKE

100 ml (3½ fl oz) passionfruit juice (approximately
  4 passionfruit)
4 egg whites (use pasteurised)
260 g (9¼ oz) caster (superfine) sugar
450 g (1 lb) unsalted butter, at room temperature
orange food colouring
2 teaspoons passionfruit seeds

23 CM (9 INCH) CAKE

160 ml (5¼ fl oz) passionfruit juice (approximately
  7 passionfruit)
7 egg whites (use pasteurised)
460 g (1 lb ½ oz) caster (superfine) sugar
675 g (1 lb 8 oz) unsalted butter, at room temperature
orange food colouring
4 teaspoons passionfruit seeds

1. Put the passionfruit juice in a saucepan over high heat and bring to the boil. Turn the heat down and simmer the juice until it has reduced by half. Remove from the heat and allow to cool.

2. Fill a saucepan one-third full of water and bring it to the boil, then turn the heat down so that the water is gently simmering. Set a heatproof bowl in the top of the saucepan, making sure that the bottom of the bowl doesn't touch the water.

3. Put the egg whites and the sugar into the bowl. Stir the mixture until all the sugar has dissolved: you should be able to rub a little of the egg white in between your thumb and fingers and not feel any grittiness from the sugar. Remove the bowl from the saucepan and transfer the egg white mixture to the bowl of a standing electric mixer (if you are using one). Using the highest setting, beat the egg whites for about 10 minutes until they are at the stiff peak stage (when you lift the beaters up a stiff peak should form; it should keep its shape and not flop over).

4. Add the butter, a small piece at a time, and beat in well. Don't worry if at some stage the mixture starts to look curdled, keep beating and the butter will incorporate into the meringue. Once all the butter has been added, beat for a few more minutes.

5. Beat in the cooled passionfruit juice.

6. If you want to create different coloured buttercream, add the orange food colouring at this stage. You should find that the fruit juice has already given a beautiful orange tone, so one cake can be left with this natural tone. Add a little bit of the food colouring at a time until you achieve the desired shade.

7. Take a portion of each of the buttercreams and mix together with the passionfruit seeds, to use as the filling for the cake. Use 150 g (5½ oz) of buttercream for the 12.5 cm (5 inch) cake, 300 g (10½ oz) for the 18 cm (7 inch) cake and 450 g (1 lb) for the 23 cm (9 inch) cake, then reserve the remainder of the buttercream for the crumb-coat and decoration.

LEMON DRIZZLE ICING

PREP: 5 minutes per batch

12.5 CM (5 INCH) CAKE
100 g (3½ oz) icing (confectioners') sugar
20 ml (½ fl oz/1 tablespoon) lemon juice

18 CM (7 INCH) CAKE
150 g (5½ oz) icing (confectioners') sugar
30 ml (1 fl oz) lemon juice

23 CM (9 INCH) CAKE
250 g (9 oz) icing (confectioners') sugar
50 ml (1¾ fl oz) lemon juice

Mix the icing sugar with the lemon juice when you are ready to use the icing.

Note   *I find it easier to make a large batch of the Swiss meringue buttercream, as it tends to mix together better. So I would advise you to make the 12.5 cm (5 inch) and 18 cm (7 inch) batches together. (Trying to make enough buttercream for all three cakes at once would probably prove too much for a domestic bowl to handle!)*

LEMON SYRUP

PREP: 5 minutes per batch

12.5 CM (5 INCH) CAKE
20 ml (½ fl oz/1 tablespoon) lemon juice
20 g (¾ oz) caster (superfine) sugar

18 CM (7 INCH) CAKE
30 ml (1 fl oz) lemon juice (roughly half a lemon)
30 g (1 oz) caster (superfine) sugar

23 CM (9 INCH) CAKE
60 ml (2 fl oz) lemon juice (roughly 1 lemon)
60 g (2 oz) caster (superfine) sugar

Prepare the lemon syrup using the method of making sugar syrup described on page 34.

PASSIONFRUIT JUICE

The best method to release all the juice from the passionfruit without incorporating any seeds is to slice the fruit in half and then scoop out all the flesh and seeds using a spoon. Put the flesh in a sieve and put the sieve on top of a bowl. Scrape the fruit through the sieve with a metal dessert spoon to extract as much pulp as possible. You really only want to see the seeds remaining in the sieve. Reserve the seeds to add to the buttercream filling.

LEVELLING AND FILLING THE CAKES

PREP: 24 hours ahead, covering the drums, 30 minutes;
10–15 minutes per cake, then 20–30 minutes chilling per cake.

EQUIPMENT

28 cm (11 inch), 23 cm (9 inch) and 18 cm (7 inch) covered
  cake drums (optional)
28 cm (11 inch), 23 cm (9 inch) and 18 cm (7 inch) thin cake
  boards
cake leveller, or cocktail sticks (toothpicks) and a serrated knife
small palette knife (I would advise investing in one for this
  project as it will make it much easier, but you can still
  achieve a desirable effect with a substitute: see page 37)
cake scraper or alternative (see page 37)
lemon syrup (see previous page)
passionfruit curd (if you cannot find this, then lemon curd
  is a perfectly acceptable alternative); you will need two
  320 g (11¼ oz) jars to fill all three cakes: 12.5 cm (5 inch),
  2 tablespoons; 18 cm (7 inch), 3 tablespoons; 23 cm
  (9 inch), 6 tablespoons

1. Level the cakes using the method described on page 37, then divide the height of the cake by three and cut the cakes using the levelling method to create three layers from each cake. Brush each layer with warm lemon syrup. Fill each cake following the method described on page 42: one layer will be filled with passionfruit curd and one layer with the seeded buttercream. Then crumb-coat each cake with the reserved buttercream (see page 45) and refrigerate for 20–30 minutes, until the buttercream has hardened.

2. Cover each cake with the remaining coloured buttercream. Use a scraper or alternative to achieve a straight-edged effect. Level the buttercream on top of the cakes as flat as possible.

3. Mix up the lemon drizzle icing: it should be runny enough to pour and create drips, but not too watery or the drips will disappear and the icing will pool at the base of the cake. Pour most of the icing on to the middle of each cake (do this one at a time). Use a palette knife (or alternative) to spread it over the top and right up to the sides; you should find drips start to form. Use the knife to control the drips, encouraging some to drip more by pulling them down a little or, if you feel a drip is dripping too far, scrape a little of it off. If there are gaps in the line of drips then pour a little more icing into the space. Leave the icing to dry: it should take a few hours to be dry enough to decorate, but overnight would be better.

DECORATING THE CAKES

PREP: 20 minutes plus 30 minutes drying time

EQUIPMENT
a spray tent or a large cardboard box
two 100 ml (3½ fl oz) cans of edible gold spray paint
15–20 pieces of fruit

For the fruit, select a mixture of large, medium and small fruits, such as pears, apples, plums, cherries, grapes, figs, physalis (cape gooseberry), strawberries, raspberries and blackberries. Apples and pears need to sit upright without toppling over and will look much better if you choose specimens that have long stems, and a leaf would be perfect (a clementine with a leaf would be brilliant)! Choose soft fruit that is slightly under-ripe and make sure that none of the fruit you use is bruised.

1. Turn the cardboard box onto its side and place the fruit inside. Spray with the edible gold paint.

2. You will find that the gold will come off on your fingers, even when it has dried, so be very careful when touching the painted fruit. If the piece has a stem use that to move it around. Allow the paint to dry, then add another layer of gold: you may need to use three layers in total to cover all the fruit skin.

3. Once the gold paint has totally dried, place the fruit on the cakes. You will find that the gold will mark the white icing, so you need to be certain of where the fruit should be placed before you start adding it. Experiment with the layout on a work surface first; this will give you the chance to move pieces around until you are happy, then transfer the fruit to the cakes.

To prevent any fruit wobbling and marking the cake add the decoration only once the cake is in situ and on a stand.

SPRAY THE FRUIT   1

Spice Up Your Life

CHOCOLATE & PEPPER COOKIES

This has been one of my all-time favourite flavour combinations since I happened across it in a magazine.

While these cookies would be the ideal accompaniment to a post-wedding breakfast coffee, how perfect would it be to serve them with a milk-based cocktail, a truly grown-up milk-and-cookies treat? I have included a cocktail recipe that will partner well with the cookies, or you could hold a party, invite some friends and create your own personalised wedding cocktail. For your younger guests an individual bottle of milk or a hot chocolate would probably be more appreciated.

'SPICE UP YOUR LIFE' AT A GLANCE

BAKING SKILL: HARD

While cookies are relatively easy to make, to create this project the cookies must be pretty much exactly the same size and depth to produce a 'cake' that doesn't topple, and this will take some experience. Alternatively you could display the cookies in bowls and then it won't be an issue. Of course if you want an easy no-bake project you can buy packaged cookies and set them in the same way out as described below.

DECORATING SKILL: EASY

The paper flowers are very easy to make and because they can be crafted in advance if you do have any issues with them you will have plenty of time to find an alternative.

The decorations for this 'cake' are made from crepe paper: you can choose colours to suit your wedding theme, or you can use real flowers if you wish, but do make sure that they are wired and taped so that you don't end up with soggy biscuits.

HOW FAR IN ADVANCE CAN IT BE MADE?

The biscuits can be made three weeks in advance and then filled with the ganache up to three days in advance. They will need to be stored in airtight containers. The flowers can be made at any time prior to setting up.

SETTING UP:

It should only take about 30 minutes to set out the cookies and place the flowers on top. The decorated 'cake' can be set up the night before the wedding if required.

PORTIONS:

156 portions (one cookie per person). You will need four batches of the cookie mixture to recreate the cookie 'cake'. If you wish to add an extra tier on the bottom of the cake you will need an extra four batches.

PRICE PER PORTION: LOW

TOTAL MAKING TIME:

Maximum of 8 hours 45 minutes plus 2½ hours for chilling.

TOTAL BAKING TIME:

Up to 3 hours, depending on how many baking trays you have.

COOKIE RECIPE

PREP: 15 minutes per batch. You will need 4 batches (312 cookies) plus 2 hours to cut out the all cookies needed and 1½ hours chilling time. If you have a standing electric mixer you can prepare two batches at once. BAKING TIME:12 minutes per tray. If you have three large trays that fit the width of your oven you can bake all the cookies in around 1 hour. If you only have one or two trays it could take you up to 3 hours. Ingredient quantities are for one batch (80 single cookies, or 40 sandwiched cookies).

----

75 g (2¾ oz) chocolate (73%)
250 g (9 oz) unsalted butter
250 g (9 oz) light brown sugar
1 egg
½ teaspoon coffee flavouring
1 teaspoon natural vanilla extract
50 g (1¾ oz) unsweetened cocoa powder
350 g (12 oz) plain (all-purpose) flour
1 teaspoon ground cinnamon
½ teaspoon flaky salt
½ teaspoon freshly ground black pepper

EQUIPMENT

large rolling pin
4 mm (³⁄₁₆ inch) spacers (see page 38) or equivalent; if the cookies are not rolled out at exactly 4 mm thickness it may affect the number of cookies that you produce, and you do need exactly 156 to produce this cake

5 cm (2 inch) round cookie cutter
small heart cutter roughly 2.5 cm (1 inch) wide (it needs to fit inside the 5 cm cookie)
baking trays: if you have large trays that will fit the width of the oven then it will be much quicker to use these. Do not place more than three trays in the oven at any one time.
baking paper

1. Melt the chocolate in a microwave or a heatproof bowl over a saucepan of simmering water and set aside to cool.

2. Beat the butter and sugar together until just combined.

3. Add the egg, coffee and vanilla extract and beat in well.

4. Beat in the melted chocolate.   »

CUTTING AND DECORATING

7

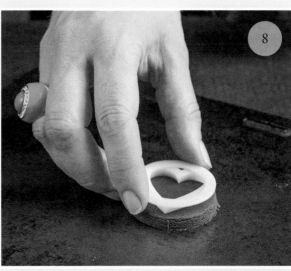

8

5. Sift the cocoa, flour and cinnamon over the chocolate mixture. Beat into the mixture along with the salt and pepper until just combined.

6. Scrape all the dough out of the mixing bowl, mould it into a flattened ball shape, wrap it in plastic wrap and chill in the refrigerator for at least an hour, preferably overnight. If you have mixed two batches at the same time divide the dough in half and wrap each separately.

7. After chilling, roll out one batch of cookie dough at a time. You may find the dough quite hard to begin with but it will soften up as you roll. To create the cookie cake you need to make sure that each cookie is the same thickness, so spacers are necessary. Cut out the cookies.

8. Press the heart cutter onto the top of each cookie (making sure that it doesn't go all the way through) and place on a baking tray lined with baking paper. Put the tray in the refrigerator to chill for 30 minutes.

9. While the cookies are chilling, preheat the oven to 200°C (400°F).

10. Put the baking tray in the oven and bake for 12 minutes (if you have hot spots in your oven you may need to turn the trays halfway through the baking time).

11. Transfer the cookies to a wire rack to cool completely, then to an airtight container.

GANACHE FILLING

PREP: 15 minutes plus 1 hour cooling

---

450 ml (15½ fl oz) thick (double) cream
650 g (1 lb 7 oz) dark chocolate (54%), chopped or buttons
1½ teaspoons natural vanilla extract
½ teaspoon coffee flavouring
½ teaspoon flaky salt
½ teaspoon pepper

1. Put the cream in a saucepan over high heat and bring to the boil.

2. Put the chocolate into a heatproof bowl and pour the boiling cream over it. Beat together until all the chocolate has melted and the elements have been totally combined.

3. Add the vanilla, coffee, salt and pepper and beat in well.

4. Leave the ganache to cool. To fill the cookies, the ganache needs to be the consistency of whipped double (thick) cream, which should be after about 1 hour of cooling. If you make the ganache in advance, store it in the refrigerator until required, then simply warm it up in a microwave on the defrost setting until it is the right consistency.

FILLING THE COOKIES

PREP: 45 minutes

EQUIPMENT
*30 cm (12 inch) disposable piping (icing) bag (optional)
cake tin, cutting board or something that has a straight
    flat bottom*

1. Fill the piping bag with the ganache, twist the top to prevent any squelching out, then cut 1 cm (⅜ inch) across the tip to create the hole.

2. Lay 5 rows of 5 cookies heart-side down on the work surface. Squirt a 3 cm (1¼ inch) blob (technical term!) of the ganache in the middle of each cookie. If you don't own a piping bag you can use an old sauce bottle (the squirty kind), making sure that it is totally clean, or you can use a teaspoon and drop a blob of the ganache on each cookie: this method can make it trickier to create an even layer of ganache.

3. Take another cookie, heart-side up, place it on top of the ganache and gently press down.

4. When all the cookies are sandwiched together, place the cake tin over the cookies and press down lightly but evenly to make all the cookies the same level. Wipe off any ganache that may have squeezed out of the edges of the cookies and then stack the cookies nearby.

5. Lay out another 25 cookies and fill and sandwich as above. As you stack these cookies next to the first batch, double-check that their heights are even.

6. When all the cookies are sandwiched and the ganache has hardened, store them in an airtight tin until required.

FILLING THE COOKIES 2

3

DECORATING

CRAFTING TIME: 1½ hours. When cutting the crepe paper strips, always cut across the grain of the crepe paper.

EQUIPMENT
scissors
hot-glue gun and two packs of glue sticks
crepe paper (colours as listed below, or different colours
  of your own choice)
3 cocktail sticks (toothpicks)

LARGE ROSETTE
4 x 16 cm (1½ x 6¼ inch) strip of white crepe paper
6 x 23 cm (2½ x 9 inch) strip of black crepe paper
7 x 45 cm (2¾ x 17¾ inch) strip of cornflower blue crepe paper
8 x 60 cm (3¼ x 24 inch) strip of light turquoise crepe paper
9 x 80 cm (3½ x 31½ inch) strip of gold crepe paper
two 13 x 115 cm (5 x 45¼ inch) strips of maroon crepe paper

1. Make vertical cuts along the white strip: make the cuts 2.5 cm (1 inch) deep and cut at 5 mm (¼ inch) intervals. Apply glue along the bottom edge of the white strip. Roll it on itself as tightly as you can.

2. Make vertical cuts along the strip of black paper: make the cuts 4.5 cm (1¾ inches) deep and cut at 5 mm (¼ inch) intervals. Apply glue along the uncut edge of the black strip and roll it around the white roll.

3. Make vertical cuts along the strip of cornflower blue paper: make the cuts 5 cm (2 inches) deep and cut at 1 cm (⅜ inch) intervals. Continue in the same manner with each of the paper strips, wrapping each new colour around the previous one.

4. Make vertical cuts along the strip of turquoise paper: make the cuts 5.5 cm (2¼ inches) deep and cut at 1 cm (⅜ inch) intervals. Apply glue and wrap as before.

5. Make vertical cuts along the gold strip: make the cuts 6 cm (2½ inch) deep and cut at 1 cm (⅜ inch) intervals.

Apply glue and wrap the paper strip around the previous layers of the rosette as before.

6. Make vertical cuts along the strips of maroon paper: make the cuts 6 cm (2½ inch) deep and cut at 1.5 cm (⅝ inch) intervals. Apply glue and wrap as before.

7. Trim the bottom of the rosette. Gently shape the rosette and fluff it out. If, like me, you have used a one-sided gold paper then turn any strips of white around so that only the gold side is showing.

MEDIUM BLUE & GOLD ROSETTE
You will need:
7 x 40 cm (2¾ x 16 inch) strip of gold crepe paper
7 x 60 cm (2¾ x 24 inch) strip of maroon crepe paper
10 x 80 cm (4 x 31½ inch) strip of light turquoise crepe paper
11 x 175 cm (4¼ x 69 inch) strip of pale blue crepe paper

1. Make vertical cuts along the strip of gold paper: make the cuts 5.5 cm (2¼ inches) deep and cut at 5 mm (¼ inch) intervals.

2. Make vertical cuts along the strip of maroon paper: make the cuts 5.5 cm (2¼ inches) deep and cut at 1 cm (⅜ inch) intervals.

3. Make vertical cuts along the strip of turquoise paper: make the cuts 7 cm (2¾ inches) deep and cut at 1 cm (⅜ inch) intervals.

4. Make vertical cuts along the strip of pale blue paper: make the cuts 2.5 cm (1 inch) deep and cut at 1 cm (⅜ inch) intervals.

5. Apply glue along the uncut edge of the gold strip. Roll it up as tightly as you can. »

6. Continue in the same manner (as for the large rosette) with all the crepe paper strips, wrapping each new colour around the previous one.

7. Trim the bottom of the rosette. Gently shape the rosette and fluff it out. If, like me, you have used a one-sided gold paper then turn any strips of white around so that only the gold side is showing.

MEDIUM BLACK-CENTRED ROSETTE

8 x 150 cm (3¼ x 59 inch) strip of black crepe paper
9 x 120 cm (3½ x 47 inch) strip of cornflower blue crepe paper
7 x 45 cm (2¾ x 17¾ inch) strip of gold crepe paper

1. Make vertical cuts along the strip of black paper: make the cuts 6 cm (2½ inches) deep and cut at 7 mm (⅜ inch) intervals.

2. Make vertical cuts along the strip of cornflower paper: make the cuts 7 cm (2¾ inches) deep and cut at 1 cm (⅜ inch) intervals.

3. Make vertical cuts along the strip of gold paper: make the cuts 4.5 cm (1¾ inches) deep and cut at 1 cm (⅜ inch) intervals.

4. Apply glue along the uncut edge of the black strip. Roll it up as tightly as you can.

5. Continue in the same manner (as for the large rosette) with all the crepe paper strips, wrapping each new colour around the previous one.

6. Trim the bottom of the rosette.

7. Gently shape the rosette and fluff it out. If, like me, you have used a one-sided gold paper then turn any strips of white around so that only the gold side is showing.

8. Place a blob of glue on the back of the rosette and insert a cocktail stick.

SMALL GOLD & MAROON ROSETTE

6 x 40 cm (2½ x 16 inch) strip of gold paper
6 x 65 cm (2½ x 25½ inch) strip of maroon crepe paper

1. Make vertical cuts along the strip of gold paper: make the cuts 4 cm (1½ inches) deep and cut at 7 mm (⅜ inch) intervals.

2. Make vertical cuts along the strip of maroon paper: make the cuts 4 cm (1½ inches) deep and cut at 7 mm (⅜ inch) intervals.

3. Apply glue along the uncut edge of the gold strip. Roll it up as tightly as you can. Apply glue along the uncut edge of the maroon strip and roll it around the gold centre.

4. Trim the bottom of the rosette. Gently shape the rosette and fluff it out. If, like me, you have used a one-sided gold paper then turn any strips of white around so that only the gold side is showing.

5. Place a blob of glue on the back of the rosette and insert a cocktail stick.

SMALL GOLD ROSETTE

6 x 140 cm (2½ x 55 inch) strip of gold paper

1. Make vertical cuts along the gold paper strip: make the cuts 4 cm (1½ inches) deep and cut at 7 mm (⅜ inch) intervals.

2. Apply glue along the uncut edge of the gold strip. Roll it up as tightly as you can.

3. Trim the bottom of the rosette. Gently shape the rosette and fluff it out. If, like me, you have used a one-sided gold paper then turn any strips of white around so that only the gold side is showing.

4. Place a blob of glue on the back of the rosette and insert a cocktail stick.

CREATING THE 'CAKE'

PREP: 15 minutes

I used a 25 cm (10 inch) cake stand as a base on which to build this cake, and the cookies fitted very snugly; however, if you are using ready-made cookies or if your cookies have spread more, then you may find that you cannot fit them all on a stand this width. You can create the cake on a covered 30 cm (12 inch) cake drum and then put that on the cake stand if you have any issues (or use a larger stand).

1. Place a vertical stack of 6 cookies in the centre of the cake stand.

2. Create a circle of 6 stacks of 6 cookies each around the middle stack.

3. Then add another circle of 12 stacks of 6 cookies around the first circle. As you are adding more cookies, keep checking on the level of the stacks: if there are any that are very different rearrange the cookies until the stacks are more level.

4. Add another stack of 6 cookies in the middle on top of the first stack.

5. Add another circle of stacks of 6 cookies around the middle stack.

6. Place the large rosette on the top of the cake; place the medium blue and gold rosette to the side, on the top of the first tier of cookies.

7. Place the gold rosette on the opposite side of the first layer to the pale blue rosette. You can stick the cocktail stick in between the cookies so that the rosette is sitting more upright.

8. Place the remaining rosettes on the bottom of the cake between the cookies and the stand. Slide the cocktail stick in between to keep the rosette in place.

STACKING THE COOKIES

2

5

COOKIES & CREAM COCKTAIL

Quantities are per person

----

40 g (1½ oz) of the ganache from the cookies, or a good-quality chocolate syrup
4 shots of milk
ice cubes
1 shot of hazelnut liqueur
1 shot of Irish cream liqueur
unsweetened cocoa powder (optional)

Note: 1 shot is approximately 45 ml (1½ fl oz).

1. Melt the ganache until it is a liquid.

2. Add 1 shot of milk and stir well together.

3. Half-fill a cocktail shaker with ice.

4. Pour in the liqueurs, the remaining milk and the ganache.

5. Seal with the lid and shake well.

6. Strain into a glass and sprinkle with a little cocoa powder, if using.

Watercolour Sunset

APPLE BLACKBERRY, CHOC CHERRY & STRAWBERRY CHAMPAGNE CAKES

There is a time during the day that photographers call the magic hour (it is also known as the golden hour).

It's just after sunrise or before sunset when the light is softer and covers everything in a golden glow. I sometimes daydream about getting married again (to the same man, of course) and we would be married at the magic hour in a woodland glade. Sometimes I even shed a tiny tear thinking about how beautiful it all would be. This cake project will be a sweet treat before you ride off into the sunset together.

'WATERCOLOUR SUNSET' AT A GLANCE

BAKING SKILL: EASY

DECORATING SKILL: EASY

(If you feel nervous about painting the watercolour then you can use decorative craft paper.)

HOW FAR IN ADVANCE CAN IT BE MADE?

Bake the layers up to five days before serving. The separate layers of the cake can be baked and then frozen up to three months before the big day. As soon as the cake has cooled wrap each layer in plastic wrap and then foil. Be careful that each layer doesn't get squashed or bashed while it is in the freezer. The cake can be layered, filled and tiered up to four days in advance. The buttercream can be made up to a week in advance and stored in the refrigerator. It can also be made up to three months in advance and frozen. Bring it to room temperature 24 hours before using and beat it to restore the texture.

The paper flower can be made at any time.

SETTING UP:

It is literally a matter of minutes to put the cake on the stand and place the flower on top. This cake will last all day once set up, depending on the temperature of your venue. It could also be set up the night before the wedding.

PORTIONS:

15 cm (6 inch), 12 portions;
20 cm (8 inch), 25 portions;
25 cm (10 inch), 46 portions.

PRICE PER PORTION: MEDIUM

TOTAL MAKING TIME:

4 hours plus 3½ hours chilling and drying.

TOTAL BAKING TIME:

Maximum 4 hours 45 minutes.

ON THE DAY:

Transport the cake to the venue in a box and add the flower after you have placed it on the cake stand or display table.

CAKE RECIPES

PREP: 20–30 minutes per layer; each tier is made up of three layers.
BAKING TIME: 25–40 minutes per layer.
Ingredient quantities are for one layer (bake three layers to create each tier).

15 CM (6 INCH) CAKE LAYER

150 g (5½ oz) strawberries, leaves removed
30 ml (1 fl oz) Champagne, prosecco or any other
*   sparkling wine*
100 g (3½ oz) unsalted butter, at room temperature
100 g (3½ oz) caster (superfine) sugar
2 large eggs, at room temperature
1 teaspoon natural vanilla extract
100 g (3½ oz) self-raising flour

1. Preheat the oven to 170°C (325°F).

2. Put the strawberries and Champagne in a saucepan over medium heat and bring to a simmer. As the strawberries cook they will start to break down; you can help this process by mashing them with a potato masher or a wooden spoon. Reduce the purée until it weighs about 55 g (2 oz). Set aside to cool.

3. Grease and line the 15 cm (6 inch) cake tin.

4. Beat the butter and sugar together until they are paler and fluffier. Add the eggs one by one (if the mixture curdles, add a teaspoon of flour).

5. Beat in the vanilla.

6. Sift the flour into the bowl and fold it into the mixture with a spoon or spatula. Fold in the strawberry purée.

7. Spoon the mixture into the prepared tin and bake for 35–40 minutes, until a skewer inserted into the centre of the cake comes out clean. Leave the cake to cool in the tin for 10 minutes, then turn it out onto a wire rack to cool completely.

20 CM (8 INCH) CAKE LAYER

200 ml (7 fl oz) water
125 g (4½ oz) good quality dark chocolate (74%)
75 g (2¾ oz) unsalted butter, cut into small pieces
1 egg
130 g (4½ oz) self-raising flour
130 g (4½ oz) light brown sugar
125 g (4½ oz) kirsch-soaked cherries (drained, juice reserved)

(Find jars of kirsch-soaked cherries in the supermarket. They are often in the dessert aisle rather than with the preserves. You can always make your own if you own a cherry tree, but you will need to make it at least six months in advance.)

1. Preheat the oven to 170°C (325°F).

2. Butter and line the 20 cm (8 inch) cake tin.

3. Put the water, chocolate and butter in a saucepan over medium heat and stir until the butter and chocolate have melted. Take the pan off the heat and set aside to cool.

4. Beat the egg in a bowl.

5. Pour in the cooled chocolate mixture and beat together.

6. Sift the flour over the chocolate mixture and shake the sugar in. Beat the mix together until all the flour and sugar is incorporated.

7. Spoon the mixture into the tin, scatter cherries over the top of the cake and bake for 30–35 minutes, until a skewer inserted into the centre of the cake comes out clean. Leave the cake to cool in the tin for 10 minutes, then turn out onto a wire rack to cool completely.

25 CM (10 INCH) CAKE LAYER

1 large cooking apple, peeled, cored and chopped
into small pieces
3 tablespoons water
200 g (7 oz) unsalted butter, at room temperature
200 g (7 oz) light brown sugar
4 eggs
200 g (7 oz) self-raising flour

(This cake is an apple cake with blackberry buttercream,
see below.)

1. Preheat the oven to 170°C (325°F).

2. Put the apple and water in a saucepan over medium heat and bring to a simmer. As the apple cooks it will start to break down; you can help this process by mashing it with a potato masher or a wooden spoon.

Reduce the purée for around 10 minutes: there should not be any obvious liquid in the pan, just apple purée. Set aside to cool.

3. Grease and line a 25 cm (10 inch) cake tin.

4. Beat the butter and sugar together until they are paler and fluffier. Add the eggs one by one (if the mixture curdles, add a teaspoon of flour).

5. Sift the flour into the bowl and fold into the mixture with a spoon or spatula. Fold in the apple purée.

6. Spoon the mixture into the cake tin and bake for 35–40 minutes, until a skewer inserted into the centre of the cake comes out clean. Leave the cake to cool in the tin for 10 minutes, then turn out onto a wire rack to cool completely.

BUTTERCREAM

PREP: 10 minutes per batch

- -

15 CM (6 INCH) CAKE

400 g (14 oz) unsalted butter, at room temperature
400 g (14 oz) icing (confectioners') sugar
4 tablespoons Champagne, prosecco or other sparkling wine

20 CM (8 INCH) CAKE

650 g (1 lb 7 oz) unsalted butter, at room temperature
650 g (1 lb 7 oz) icing (confectioners') sugar
8 tablespoons of the reserved kirsch syrup from the cherries

25 CM (10 INCH) CAKE

900 g (2 lb) unsalted butter, at room temperature
900 g (2 lb) icing (confectioners') sugar
150 g (5½ oz) blackberry jelly (if you cannot source jelly,
then use blackberry jam and strain out the pips)
dusky pink food colouring

1. Beat the butter until it is pale and fluffy.

2. Add the icing sugar and beat well.

3. Add the flavouring and beat well. If the mixture separates and curdles add more icing sugar and keep beating until everything comes together.

4. Colour the blackberry icing pink with the food colouring. It needs to be a tone darker than the cherry buttercream.

5. Separate out 200 g (7 oz) of the blackberry icing and add more food colouring until it turns a dark pink.

LAYERING AND ASSEMBLING THE TIERS

PREP: 24 hours ahead, covering the drum, 10 minutes; 10–15 minutes per tier plus 20–30 minutes chilling time

EQUIPMENT

30 cm (12 inch), 25 cm (10 inch) and 20 cm (8 inch) cake boards (uncovered for crumb coating)
covered 30 cm (12 inch) cake drum (see page 41 for details: you may wish to colour the fondant to match the darkest buttercream), optional
20 cm (8 inch) and 15 cm (6 inch) thin cake boards
cake leveller or large serrated knife and cocktail sticks (toothpicks)
palette knife (or alternative, see page 37)
cake scraper (or alternative, see page 37)
spirit level (optional)
1 large spoonful of strawberry jam (for the 15 cm cake)
3 large spoonfuls of cherry jam (for the 20 cm cake)
7 large spoonfuls of blackberry jelly (for the 25 cm cake)
syrup (see right)

1. Level the layers using the method described on page 37. Fill the tiers using the method described on page 42: one layer will be filled with jam and the other with a 1 cm (⅜ inch) deep layer of buttercream. Remember to place the bottom layer of the 15 cm (6 inch) and 20 cm (8 inch) cakes on the thin cake boards before you start filling.

2. Crumb-coat each tier using the method describe on page 45 and refrigerate for 20–30 minutes, until the buttercream has hardened.

SYRUP

PREP: 5 minutes

15 CM (6 INCH) CAKE
25 ml (1 fl oz) Champagne, prosecco or sparkling wine
25 g (1 oz) caster (superfine) sugar
20 CM (8 INCH) CAKE
90 ml (3 fl oz) reserved kirsch syrup from the cherries
25 CM (10 INCH) CAKE
75 ml (2¼ fl oz) water
75 g (2¾ oz) caster (superfine) sugar

Make the flavoured syrup for each tier, following the method for making sugar syrup described on page 34.

BUTTERCREAM 5

COVERING & ASSEMBLING THE CAKE

PREP: 10–15 minutes per tier

1. Set aside 75 g (2¾ oz) of the paler-coloured blackberry icing. Apply a thick layer of the blackberry-flavoured buttercream to the 25 cm (10 inch) apple cake. You will not need to layer as much on the top of the cake as on the sides; if you do, the frosting may start to bulge up once you have merged the tiers, so add just enough to cover the crumb-coat and enable you to incorporate some texture. Spend a little time achieving a balanced texture around the cake using the palette knife, then finally use the scraper (or alternative) to create a straight edge around the sides.

2. Set aside 50 g (1¾ oz) of the cherry-flavoured buttercream. Cover the 20 cm (8 inch) cake with the remaining cherry-flavoured buttercream in the same manner as described in step 1.

3. Cover the 15 cm (6 inch) cake with the Champagne-flavoured buttercream in the same manner as described in step 1.

4. Dowel the 25 cm (10 inch) and 20 cm (8 inch) tiers using the method described on page 50, then place the tiers on top of each other.

5. Use the palette knife to add a layer of the darker-coloured blackberry buttercream around the bottom tier, covering roughly half the side. Use the scraper to smooth this over so that the two colours start to merge.

6. Add a line of the reserved blackberry buttercream around the bottom of the middle tier, using the same method as step 5. Make sure to hide any gaps between the tiers.

7. Add a line of the reserved cherry buttercream around the bottom of the top tier, using the same method as step 5.

8. Store in a cool dry environment (this cake can be stored in a refrigerator if required.)

OMBRE ICING EFFECT

1

2

DECORATION

CRAFTING TIME: 45 minutes, plus 2 hours drying time

EQUIPMENT

27 x 73 cm (10¾ x 28¾ inch) sheet of watercolour paper
large 5 cm (2 inch) watercolour wash brush (alternatively, you could use a soft-bristled decorating brush)
2 cm (¾ inch) square-tipped paintbrush
pink and purple watercolours
container of water
gummed paper tape (kraft paper tape)
templates (see page 227)
scissors
hot-glue gun and 1 packet of glue sticks (or craft glue of your choice)
maroon crepe paper (or tissue paper)
black flower stamens
lollipop stick or long skewer

1. You need to stretch the watercolour paper first. This will prevent any crinkles and keep the petals nice and flat. Lay the paper on a table or large board. Wet the gummed paper tape using a wash brush.

2. Stick down the watercolour paper with the gummed paper tape, making sure that you tape down every bit of the edges.

3. Use the wash brush to wash a layer of water all over the paper. It needs to be fairly wet, but if there are pools of water forming on the surface then dab these off with the large brush or some paper towel.

4. Mix the purple and pink paints together to create a plum colour. With the square brush add a stripe of colour at the top and bottom edges of the paper (see page 222). Blend the colour into the water to create an ombre effect. Watercolour paint will lighten as it dries, so you may need to add some stronger colour to the very edges of the ombre strip.

5. Once the shine of the water has disappeared and the colour is nearly dry to the touch, add some splashes and flicks of paint using the square-tipped brush. >>

PREPARING THE PAPER

1

2

6. Leave the paper to dry out completely: this could take a couple of hours depending on the temperature of the room, but you can speed things up by drying it with a hair dryer.

7. Remove the paper from the board or table. Cut out the petals from the paper. Align the bottom of the petal templates along the edges on the darker stripes of colour. To create one large flower you will need: 7 large petals; 6 medium petals; 6 small petals; and 1 circle for the back.

8. To make the flower centre, scrunch up some crepe paper to make a ball that is roughly 2.5 cm (1 inch) in diameter.

9. Cut a 9 cm (3½ inch) square of crepe paper, cover the ball with the paper, press the top down on the work surface to flatten it slightly, then cut off any excess paper at the back and secure it with a blob of glue.

10. Glue the black stamens to the back of the flower centre.

11. Cut the slits down the centre of each petal as indicated in the templates.

12. Apply a little glue down one side of the slit on each of the petals. Overlap this with the other side of the petal and press together until the glue holds.

13. Take three of the smallest petals and glue them together in the centres to form a shape like a short, fat propeller. Glue another small petal on the back of the 'propeller' in the space between two petals. Repeat this process with the remaining two petals to form a circular arrangement of six overlapping petals.

14. Glue a medium-size petal to the back of the flower with the bottom aligned halfway up the first row of petals, and offset so that the broader part of the medium petal is in a gap in the first round. Add the rest of the petals in this round, overlapping them slightly.

15. Glue the large petals to the back of the flower to form a third row, in the same manner as the second. Glue the centre with the stamens into the middle of the flower.

16. Glue the lollipop stick to the back of the flower and glue the circle over it. Place the flower on the cake using the lollipop stick to secure it.

PAINTING THE PAPER

4

5

TEMPLATES

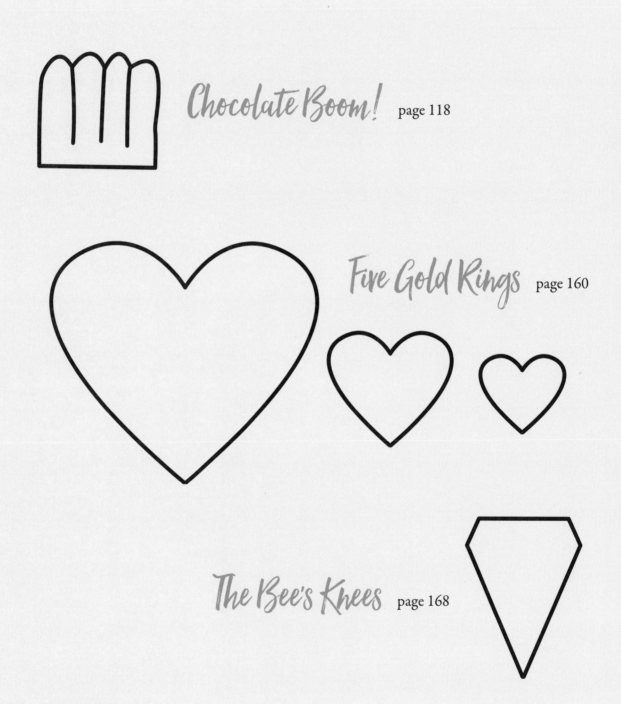

Chocolate Boom! page 118

Five Gold Rings page 160

The Bee's Knees page 168

Watercolour Sunset page 214

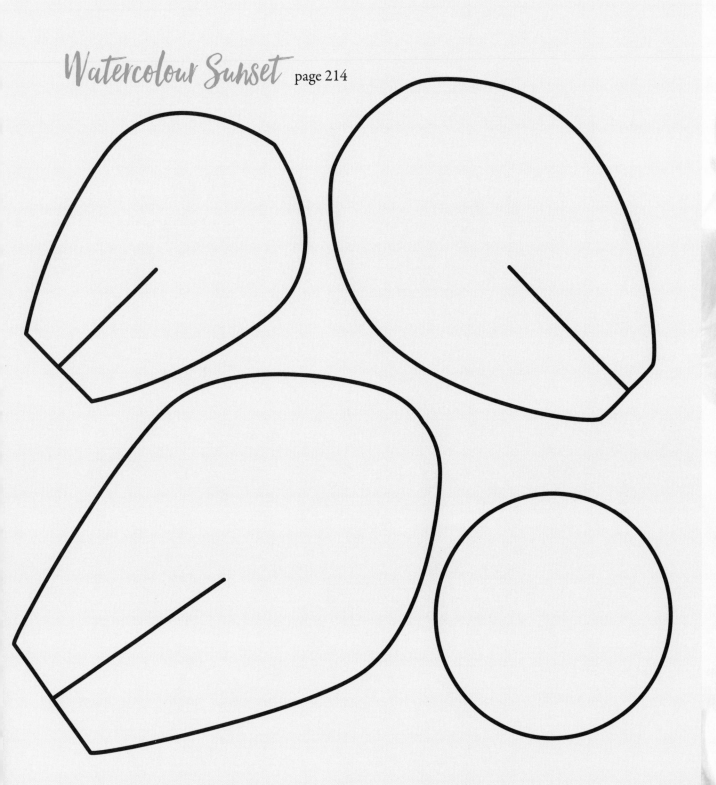

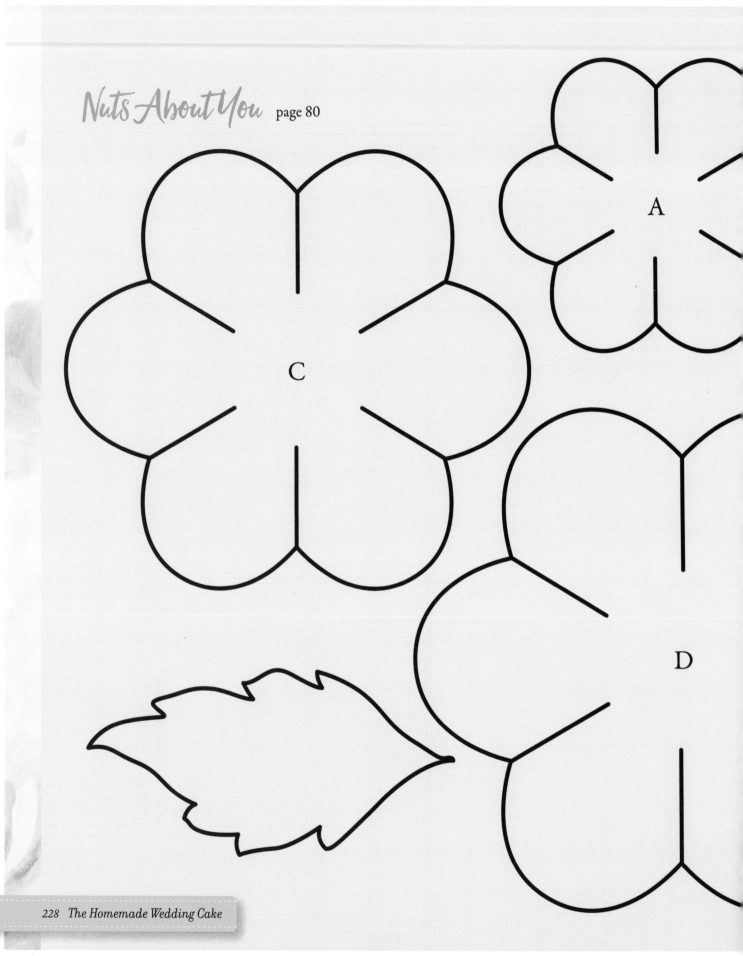

E

B

Suppliers List

While this is by no means a comprehensive list of suppliers, I can give you an overview of suppliers and brands that I use. Most of these will be available online if you cannot find them at your local cake-decorating supplier, or most suppliers will be able to offer you a suitable alternative.

CAKE TINS – The cake tins I prefer are Invicta, a UK-based company. Buy a professional-quality tin if your budget allows. Nordic Ware produce traditional bundt tins, but I used a Dr Oetker silicone tin for the Five Gold Rings.

BAKING INGREDIENTS – I buy these from my local supermarket.

COUVERTURE CHOCOLATE – I use Callebaut which is readily available worldwide, and online from Amazon. Valrhona is another brand that many chefs use.

LAVENDER – Edible lavender or culinary lavender is available from www.souschef.co.uk and they ship across Europe. You will also find it in online stores worldwide.

PASTEURISED EGG WHITES – I love the Two Chicks brand in the UK. You may find pasteurised egg whites in the freezer section of large supermarkets.

WAFER PAPER – You can find this on Amazon or www.cakesaroundtown.com.au

FOOD COLOURING – There are many great brands that you can use: AmeriColor, Sugarflair, Squires or Wilton, to name a few. I have used Sugarflair colours in these projects. The professional brands will have a larger selection of more subtle colours than the supermarket variety.

EDIBLE GOLD SPRAY PAINT – the best one I have found is PME Edible Lustre Spray.

EDIBLE-INK PENS – I used Rainbow Dust colour pens to create the Key Largo project.

EDIBLE METALLIC PAINT – I always use Rainbow Dust metallic food paints; dark gold and dark silver are the colours I prefer to use.

VINTAGE FABRIC – I am fortunate to have a mother who hoards fabric, so I raid her cupboards for my projects: if you are not so lucky try thelinengarden.blogspot.co.uk. Vicky Trainor curates this treasure trove of an online shop. In Australia, try www.vintagefabrics.com.au.

BISCUIT TINS – I have used Tala biscuit tins for the 'Love-in-a-box' project; these are available from homewares stores and department stores worldwide.

FLOWER AND LEAF CUTTERS – I have used PME brand cutters for these projects.

CAKE STANDS AND STYLING – Two of my favourite stores are www.bakerandmaker.com and boutique.borrowedbluewedding.com, both of which deliver internationally, although you may find their products in online stores local to you. My favourite cake stands are milk glass, available in a wide variety of sizes and colours that will make any cake look more special. They are made in the US but most countries will have an importer and supplier.

POMPOMS – I love a pompom and there are some great tissue-paper pompom makers on sites such as Etsy. Etsy is a great site to use, as it will find a supplier local to your area or country. www.pompomblossom.com will rent out their beautiful giant pompoms for events.

CAKE TOPPERS – search sites such as Etsy and Folksy to find a supplier who will make a custom topper for your cake.

Index

Entries in *italics* indicate projects.

Thank You

As at any traditional wedding I have to end here with a plethora of thank yous and acknowledgments to the people without whom this book would never have been written.

Thank you to my agent Claire Hulton, who has been invaluable in helping make this romantic dream a reality.

It was a pleasure to work with the delightful people at Murdoch Books again. I have to especially thank Diana Hill, my fabulous publisher whom I think of as my chief bridesmaid: she is a genius at making a lowly author feel capable! She has been assisted by the fabulous Emma Hutchinson, who led me through the whole process, making it very easy, and the lovely Hugh Ford and Melody Lord. Thanks too, to Sarah Odgers and Tania Gomez for the book design. A big thank you to Clive Kintoff and Jemma Crocker also, for all their support. You have all helped to make this a delightful book to create.

Every wedding needs a photographer and I am privileged to have been able to work with Nathan Pask again. You are a dream to work with and nail it every time!

Thank you to Snap Studios for looking after us so well.

Flowers are an integral part of a wedding and I got some great advice from May Mackay from Petals, Berkhamsted, UK. I also need to thank my friends and neighbours who let me strip their gardens of flowers and greenery.

I have to thank some wonderful suppliers for helping me source lovely props to style all the projects: Bee from Gilded Linens for the loan of some gorgeous table linens, Vicky Trainer from The Linen Garden for some lovely cloths and lacy bits, Amy from The Paper Emporium for gorgeous confetti and tassels, Sophie from Pompom Blossom for the amazing pompoms and tassels, and Katherine from Borrowed Blue for the wonderful cake stands. Thanks to all my friends who lent me plates, bowls, stands and anything else I could swipe from their houses.

I also took over some houses for the photoshoot, so there is a big thank you that I have to say to Jo, Hannah and Annamarie, you were all very patient.

Thank you to all my gorgeous models who gave up their time to pose with cakes! Erica, James, Kaitlin, Jo, Stephanie, Lexie, Sadie, Leah, Hannah, Trish, Lizz, Naomi, Lydia, Paul, Simon, Nell and Ali. And I cannot forget my fabulous little bridesmaids and pageboys: Archie, Jackie, Darcy, Amelie and Genevieve. You were all amazing and sooo scrumptious!

One of the downsides of being a full-time cake maker is that you never have photo-ready nails. They always need some TLC to make them presentable, so thanks go to Sharon Herholdt for her amazing nail work. Thanks also to Rebecca Whitworth for stepping in at the last minute as an amazing make-up artist for my gorgeous models.

There are also many, many friends who deserve a special thank you for helping me out while I was writing the book, especially for looking after my kidlets while I was up to my eyes in buttercream. And to my mum and Del who came to look after my kidlets during the photoshoots.

Marriage can be a tricky business and it takes work. I am fortunate to have learnt from an amazing couple, my mum and dad. Thank you for being so supportive of me and my own little family. Thanks to my dad for making the lovely cake stands for the 'Five Gold Rings' project and to my mum for letting me raid her cupboards for props.

I want to thank my lovely girls, Amelie and Genevieve, for all their help and support; especially to Amelie for letting me utilise her crafting skill in making props. I love you both to bits.

Of course a wedding wouldn't be a wedding without a groom, and my own leading man is Paul, who has supported me in all my endeavors with good humour and grace. He even bravely stepped in when I lost one of my models. Thank you for always being there for me and I promise not to feed you too much cake from now on!

Natasha

Published in 2016 by Murdoch Books, an imprint of Allen & Unwin

Murdoch Books Australia
83 Alexander Street
Crows Nest NSW 2065
Phone: +61 (0) 2 8425 0100
Fax: +61 (0) 2 9906 2218
murdochbooks.com.au
info@murdochbooks.com.au

Murdoch Books UK
Ormond House
26–27 Boswell Street
London WC1N 3JZ
Phone: +44 (0) 20 8785 5995
murdochbooks.co.uk
info@murdochbooks.co.uk

For Corporate Orders & Custom Publishing contact our business development team at
salesenquiries@murdochbooks.com.au.

Publisher: Diana Hill
Editorial Manager: Emma Hutchinson
Design Managers: Hugh Ford and Emily O'Neill
Project Editor: Melody Lord
Design Concept and Layout: Sarah Odgers
Design Concept Development: Tania Gomez
Photographer: Nathan Pask
Food Preparation and Styling: Natasha Collins
Production Manager: Alexandra Gonzalez

A cataloguing-in-publication entry is available from the catalogue of the
National Library of Australia at nla.gov.au.

ISBN 978 1 74336 624 0 Australia
ISBN 978 1 74336 692 9 UK

A catalogue record for this book is available from the British Library.

Colour reproduction by Splitting Image Colour Studio Pty Ltd, Clayton, Victoria
Printed by 1010 Printing International Limited, China